PRAISE FOR THE E

"Those who read this book [...] Tim Phillips. Read it. Dige[...] [...] well informed and find yourself a better student of the subject at the end."
—**Robert Duvall, Academy Award-winning actor, *Tender Mercies*, Emmy Award-winning actor, *Broken Trail*, writer, director, and producer**

"An instructive, no nonsense, passionate cry to the actor: Bring your intelligence and humanity to the audition *not* your desperation."
—**Larry Moss, acting coach and director, author of *Intent to Live***

"Tim provides a boot camp for actors that retrains us, redirects us to become hunters for truth in our work. The end result is that you remember that the result is irrelevant and immaterial as it relates to getting a job or mastering a take. You remember that living truthfully in the world of the script is everything and is always achievable. And when that is achieved, the rest will take care of itself. Always."
—**Richard Schiff, Emmy Award-winning actor, *The West Wing***

"Audition for Your Career, Not the Job" has the power to shift your way of being to one that's curious, open to love, intuitively confident, and, ultimately, human. Imagine facing your next audition with a 'Put me in Coach—I've got this!' feeling. That is the gift of this book."
—**Kim Hudson, script consultant and author of *The Virgin's Promise***

"Tim Phillips' style of teaching fosters great respect for the work and for each other."
—**Wendie Malick, Emmy Award-nominated actress, *Just Shoot Me!***

"I've come to think of Tim Phillips as 'The Wizard.' I've worked for several years with Tim as my coach and teacher. His deep instinct to follow clues of language, emotion, and tone invariably leads actors into a place they're not aware they know about. Yet, by session's end, they are certain they not only know it, but are at home in this place: the soul of the character. Tim Phillips is a master for anyone working on stage or in television and film."
—**Robert Wisdom, actor *The Wire, Burn Notice, Prison Break,* and *Happy Town***

"Tim Phillips is to auditions what Sanford Meisner is to acting. No joke, this guy is the real deal. I've doubled my booking ratios since working with him!"
—**James DuMont, actor**

"After working for many years in Mexico, I needed to understand how American auditions worked. Auditioning was not my 'thing.' With Tim I learned not only to get where I wanted to be emotionally, but to get there fast and with very little information. As a result, I now enjoy auditioning a lot! Tim is sharp and accurate, and he loves actors."
—**Kate del Castillo, actress**

"Tim Phillips is the *crème de la crème* when it comes to teaching actors the craft of auditioning. If you don't know what this man has discovered about this crucial process, you may be unknowingly digging yourself an unfortunate hole that lasts ten years or longer. But don't despair. Learn from this pioneer today and you can easily have auditioning success now!"
—**Robert and Michelle Colt, Acting Success Now**

"Tim is the acting teacher for professionals, the teacher that takes you to the next step. As a casting director, when I audition an actor who has studied with Tim, I see they know how to find a connection to the material and have the confidence to use it in their work. That's often the difference between being a good actor and a working actor."
—**Nora Brennan, Nora Brennan Casting**

"Tim Phillips is inspiring and electric! He gave me a gift that I rely on both as a teacher and actress, how to 'Sherlock Holmes' the text and connect to the truth and beauty of the world of the script. His work defies gravity and lifts actors to a place where they can meet their full potential as an artist."
—**Janice Orlandi, Artistic Director, Actors Movement Studio**

"I am a big fan of Tim."
—**Brian O'Neil, author of** *Actors Take Action* **and** *Acting as a Business*

"Tim has taken my auditions to a whole new level. Since working with him, I've booked over 90 percent of the roles I've read for, including a recurring role on *Weeds,* a guest spot on *Bones* and supporting leads in three studio films. He has led me to more interesting and specific choices, which I know has separated me from everyone else being seen. The guy is great!"
—**Bruce Nozick, actor,** *Weeds*

"What can I say? Tim Phillips is simply the best acting teacher I've ever studied under. In my career, the only tools that have ever proven workable for television's fast pace are the ones I learned from Tim."
—**Beth Chamberlin, actress,** *Guiding Light*

Audition for Your Career, Not the Job

MASTERING THE ON-CAMERA AUDITION

TIM PHILLIPS
WITH STEPHANIE GUNNING

Tim Phillips Studio
Los Angeles, California

Sherlock Holmesing the Text® is a trademarked process.

Tim Phillips Studio
2124 S. Redondo Blvd.
Los Angeles, CA. 90016

For information about special discounts for bulk purchases, please contact Tim Phillips Studio at (310) 772-8262 or assistant@timphillipsstudio.com.

Cover design by Emily Furlani
Interior design by Shaila Abdullah

ISBN: 978-0-615-32846-1
Library of Congress Control Number: 2011960252

To Elssa and Sara

CONTENTS

INTRODUCTION

The phone rings, an email arrives, your smart phone vibrates. It's your agent. A project is being cast and there's a part in it that might be right for you. They're expecting you at the casting office tomorrow. You don't have a whole lot of time, but that's okay. Opportunity has just come knocking at your front door and you know you have the chops to open it. After all, that's what you do... you're an actor. This is your chance to act.

Perhaps you intend to self-submit a video of yourself doing an audition for a role you saw posted online. This happens more and more often these days. You are taking control of your destiny as an artist.

In any case, the "sides" either arrive or you download them. Now you've got a few pages of script in hand along with a short description of the character and the scene: a name, a place, and a few other pertinent facts. It's time to put your training and talent and energy to good use. Your task is to transform those words on the page into a memorable living and breathing human being.

What's the first thought that goes through your mind? Is it negative or positive?

"Boy, I really want to book this one. I could use the money from this job."

"I wonder who I'm up against. I hope they like me. I thought my last audition was solid; but I never heard anything… I don't want that to happen again."

"Wahoo! It's playtime. I can't wait! Who do I get to be?"

"Let's get down to business."

You've got a big audition lined up for a role in a film or on a television series. What do you do now? This book covers steps you can take and specific skills you can put to use right away so that you will feel more confident about your performance in your next audition and make a great and lasting impression on casting directors and producers. If your work is consistently first-rate and memorable, every on-camera audition like this one becomes an opportunity to advance your acting career.

Most actors are theatre-trained and love the whole process of performing on stage. Believe me, I appreciate the lure. That's my background, too. Before becoming a master teacher, I was a theatre actor for years. Even after having shot films with great actors like Robert Duvall and Meryl Streep (okay, that scene ended up on the cutting room floor), I never loved it as much as I have loved being on stage. Do you feel the same way?

Of course, there's a catch. As a theatre actor, I mostly earned my living from tending bar. The plain truth was then, and is more so now, that doing theatre is not as lucrative for actors as doing film and television. So here's the deal, first you learn how to make a living by auditioning well for film and television. Make money. Then you can afford to do what you want to do in theatre. And if you love doing film and television, that's great!

While we know that you would like to book the job you're auditioning for (both for the money, and for the chance to act and do what you love), if you're like many actors, you could drive yourself crazy trying to figure out what the producers, casting directors, and writers want for the part and ways you could be more pleasing. You could easily get distracted. In a high-pressure situation like this, it's most important to be prepared, relax, and concentrate on the one thing that's under your control: you and your performance.

If you do everything in your power to ensure that you do your best work, afterwards you can step out of the audition room, pat yourself on the back for a job well done, leave the day's audition behind you, and move on to prepare for the next audition. You might get brought back for this role… or not. You might get feedback… or not. Many factors go into the selection of an actor for a specific role, and you may never know how the decision for any given project was made. That's why, for actors, it's crucial to stay ready for the next call. You have to be able to raise your spirits and then focus like a laser in the moment with no barriers against expressing your humanity.

Let the deciders decide. That's their function, not yours. You're here to act. Why? Because you love it. And, yes to make money—but there are easier ways to do that. I think you and I could agree that you do this out of love for the craft.

I suggest you adopt a long-term view. Adopt the attitude of "Next!" Make it your philosophy to *audition for your career, not the job*. Have fun. Enjoy your moments to shine. Be intent on crafting the best performance you can with the few pages of the script you've been provided, and let your high-quality auditions serve as your calling card. Even if you do not get the job you audition for today, you can still prove to the people who make the casting decisions that you'd be a valuable asset tomorrow.

One day, you'll book a role. You'll deliver on your promise. A paycheck will come. Then, go back and do theatre if you still want to do it. You'll decide what's next!

Be Professional, Be Yourself

The quality of your work is the only thing under your control, and it's important to approach your work in a way that feels fun and rewarding. If you learn the habits described in this book, the possibility of not being chosen literally won't be able to shake your confidence before, during, or after an audition; and you won't suffer over time from burnout or begin feeling miserable and rejected. As Michael Chiklis, lead actor from *The Shield* and *No Ordinary Family,* says of the casting process, "It's not rejection. It's selection."[1]

The idea is to set your own performance goals and determine for yourself whether or not you have met them. Then ghosts of "might have been," "could have been," "If only I had…," or "Damn it, I sounded better in the car… in the shower… when I was reading with my friend" won't haunt you. Your focus instead will be on perfecting the elements of your craft. Remember, an acting career is a marathon, not a sprint. Next!

Creative teams that produce and cast film and TV productions want to work with actors they can trust to get the job done. Professionalism as an actor means showing up prepared to deliver the goods on the spur of the moment and under great pressure. That includes being on time for your audition and every subsequent engagement. They need to know that you care enough to take your work seriously. A lot of money is on the line whenever shooting is taking place— and they are always mindful of it. Your audition is a chance to show them that you are capable both of crafting an interesting human being and of discovering and developing the life of this character from the screenplay. They want to see how you would handle the role *if it were yours today.*

What would you bring to this role that no one else could or did bring? Ideally, that's what your audition reveals. Tall, short, dark-skinned, light-skinned, young or old, high-pitched voice, low-pitched voice—some aspects of being are beyond transformation. But what's interesting about you on film is not just your appearance; it's also the information that your life has written into your body, which emerges from your crafting while you're performing. Audiences like to watch the combination of you and your crafting.

My definition of acting is *being human in a human circumstance.* When you begin to implement the techniques you'll read about in this book, you'll actually relax, be natural, and discover more interesting human behavior in front of the camera. After all, you are a human being already. You don't have far to go! You're halfway to getting this job already. You just have to build an imaginative bridge between your own life and the life of the character you're being asked to portray.

If you haven't studied acting yet, it is essential to find a teacher who can introduce you to the basic tools of acting. There are many methods and teachers to choose from; some are similar, some are not, but all lead to being capable on command of doing what an ordinary child of four instinctually does all day long, which is to play, daydream, and express what it would be like to be this or that person (or tree, dog, cloud, banana, chimpanzee, extra-terrestrial… and so on). For twenty years, I lived in New York and taught auditioning based upon The Meisner Technique, as a means for actors to live truthfully under imaginary circumstances. Following a move to Los Angeles, I developed the advanced approach to on-camera auditioning you are holding in your hands right now.

This book does not offer basic instruction in acting. It is geared towards aspiring professional actors who have studied and are ready to audition because they feel prepared to deliver the goods on a film set or television sound stage. That being said, I believe in actors receiving training no matter how talented they are. If they want to compete, they must attend technique and scene study classes in order to hone and refresh their skills. For the same reason, even longtime professionals seek advice from coaches. Needing expert coaching is as true for actors as it is for athletes and businesspeople. Even after actors finish their initial training, they need to continuously practice and refine their skills; anything they can do to stand out as *special* helps them.

If you keep working on your craft persistently, you will be in the position to out-craft the best buddy of the director or the producer's girlfriend when your shot at a role comes.

You'll also be ready to out-craft well-known, highly-skilled performers. For certain, you'll be able to level the playing field. That's the real point of all this.

The Camera Knows

Acting for the camera is different than stage acting. For one thing, it is much more intimate, which means the size of a performance has to be scaled for a narrower perspective. The frame of a camera in an audition setting is a picture frame that captures your head, arms, and upper torso. There is no need to shout or gesture broadly to be seen or heard by someone sitting yards away, as they would be seated in the back of a theatre. Furthermore, the camera is a neutral observer. It records everything it sees and censors nothing. It reveals knowledge. If you are ambivalent or uncertain about the meaning of a line you're saying, or if you haven't made clear decisions about what you want, the stakes and urgency, and your relationship with the person you're speaking to, the camera shows it. It's an X-ray, if you will, that reveals only what is there.

In an on-camera audition, the text an actor works with is the script of a short scene (usually only a few pages long), which is drawn from the screenplay and commonly referred to as the *sides*. Sometimes you get multiple scenes. The actor's first task before every performance—and an audition should definitely be viewed as a performance—is *finding the human being, and the circumstance that the human being finds him or herself in, within the text*.

An actor's second task before a performance is to do everything possible to fuse him or herself and the character, so the performance is the actor *living the life of the character truthfully.* (For our purposes here, the word "actor" refers to males and females alike.)

Working in film or television is a lot like auditioning in that you sit around on the set or in your trailer for hours and then, suddenly, they want you *now!* At that moment, you're expected to be ready to work. No one cares how late you were out the night before. No one cares if you're concerned about something going on at home. You've got to come out and do your two or more takes, possibly from various angles. You must be ready the minute the camera turns on. And if the director or a leading actor wants to do twenty takes of the same scene, you have to be able to deliver essentially the same performance consistently twenty times. You have to be prepared.

My goal is to help you develop your audition skills to the highest possible level by giving you all the tools you need for crafting successfully, pulling massive amounts of information from the sides very quickly, and delivering a performance even under pressure.

You Just Need the Right Tools

I now live and run an acting studio in Los Angeles and teach in New York one weekend each month. Several years ago, when I was still based in New York City full time, I owned a cabin in the woods. One weekend, a friend came up to visit. We were hanging out fishing and drinking beers for a while. Then I took him to the backyard to show him my new tool shed. By that point, I needed two sheds to hold my tools for gardening and fixing things around the place. When the first shed got full, I went out and bought the second one.

I thought it was cool. My friend was duly impressed. "Holy cow, Tim, you sure have a lot of tools!" he exclaimed. But then he shook his head from side to side in dismay and told me, "You know, I don't buy tools. It's kind of a principle with me."

"What do you mean?" I asked.

"Well, if you buy tools, you have to use them," he said, laughing.

The reason I'm telling you this story is not to point out that my friend was lazy (although he might have been). He just didn't share my passion for puttering. He wasn't interested in planting a garden and he didn't have a leaky roof to repair. He had no ambitions that would require him to own tools, and he liked it that way.

The fact that you are reading this book tells me two things about you that would distinguish you from my friend. First, you have an ambition of some kind… as an actor. Second, you're not yet getting the results you want from your auditions and you are seeking guidance. It's possible that you're being seen, but not being called back. Or you're being called back, but you're not getting cast. It's clear you take your career seriously because you're actively looking for tools, inspiration, and guidance that can change your results and help you live out your dreams of being a professional actor.

In *Audition for Your Career, Not the Job*, I am offering you the equivalent of a full shed of tools for acting on camera. But it is important for you to understand that these tools won't work for you—they simply won't help you to achieve your desired results—unless you "buy" into these ideas and then use them. If you are willing to apply these tools to the craft of acting and practice them regularly (meaning on a near-daily basis), you'll soon get so good at integrating them into your audition performances that not only will the quality of your work improve, you will also be able to apply them and adjust your performance quickly and effectively on the spot or when you're under pressure. This will become so ingrained in you that it will feel like second nature.

Once you can produce high-quality acting on the spur of the moment (as is always necessary in an audition setting) you can be confident that you will capture the attention of casting directors, directors, and producers. You may not get every job you go after, but you'll get some jobs. When the right part for you comes along, the people who have seen your work will give you a shot at winning the role. That's why I encourage you to shift the focus away from getting a job to inhabiting the character, this *human being,* as fully as possible. Do it for yourself. Aim for producing superb performances over and over again. It's important to recognize that this will require patience and practice.

According to social commentator Malcolm Gladwell, "Ideas and products and messages and behaviors spread just like viruses do."[2] In his book *The Tipping Point* (Back Bay Books, 2002), he explains how "contagiousness" occurs among groups of people. You want your career to be like an epidemic, for it to hit a tipping point where *suddenly you're the commodity in high demand and you are prepared to capitalize on the moment of opportunity.* That can occur by showing up and doing good work every time. Even if you don't get the first, second, or third job you audition for, be consistent and solid. The quality of your work will be influential in bringing you back to the casting directors' attention. Casting directors understand quality when they see it. And their role in the production process is to bring the right actors to the attention of producers and directors.

Always give "good audition."

Little things make a big difference is the message of Gladwell's book, and I've found that principle to be true for auditions. Making clear and specific choices on every single line of a scene about every little thing underlying your character's human behavior adds up. Five minutes of quality work in an audition setting can lead to a lifetime of opportunity for a professional film, television, and stage actor.

How this Book Is Organized

Over the years, I invented a way of reading sides from a screenplay or play (dialogue from your potential role) that enables you to suck up all the information you need in order to craft an audition performance *in one reading*. So you can do it quickly. If you have four pages of dialogue and only fifteen minutes to prepare your role, with these techniques you could spend a minute per page sucking up information, and then spend the other ten minutes crafting the piece so that you would become the character inside the scene instead of remaining a member of the audience. It is essential that you inhabit the human being you're portraying during the audition as fully as possible. For after all, this is a clear indication of what you would be like to work with on a set.

Among other things, being fully prepared means you have the ability to respond to a director's adjustments on the spur of the moment in an audition without losing your way through the material. You have legs to stand on, which gives you freedom to be human. I've seen unknown actors cast if a director fought for them to get the job. It happens.

Audition for Your Career, Not the Job is organized in two main parts. Part One, "Sherlock Holmesing the Text®" teaches my process for how to quickly grab information from the sides. This is something that can only be done with a script in hand. To be a successful actor, you must be a good detective. There are three essential tools that a good detective has, which a good actor also possesses: curiosity, intuition, and deductive reasoning. In the chapters of Part One, we'll consider how these three tools can help you be successful in various phases of the process of rapid script analysis.

Part Two, "Crafting Your Butt Off," teaches you how to draw forth a character from your own limitless imagination. Some of the work of crafting can only be done with particular sides in hand. Some really should be done on a daily basis, because it will benefit you in more than one audition. Being fully prepared to audition *to please yourself* is not something that most actors are capable of doing, or comfortable doing, on the spur of the moment. The acting skills most actors need can only be developed through years of ongoing self-exploration and play, through repetition, relaxation, and reflection.

In order to be well prepared for an audition, having the ability both to deductively reason your way through the script and to craft your role from the sides is necessary.

Have I Piqued Your Interest Yet?

During the past twenty-five-plus years, I have personally coached over thirty-five thousand auditions. Approximately 70 percent of my current students book the auditions that they bring into my classes to prepare at the Tim Phillips Studios (visit us on the Web at TimPhillipsStudio.com) in Los Angeles and New York City. You could say, therefore, that the steps described in this book produce reliable results. It has been the experience of the thousands of students and actors I coach individually that their careers begin to heat up or explode after they begin working in the manner I teach. Casting directors start bringing these actors in for more auditions, they are called back more frequently for second- and third-round auditions, and producers and directors begin to hire them regularly. The level of their achievement skyrockets.

The same can happen for you.

So, my promise to you is this: If you follow my advice in this book, as it is written—including practicing the exercises—this book will positively change your on-camera auditions by teaching you skills that improve your ability to read and interpret the sides quickly, helping you to trust your instincts and make strong, bold, specific acting choices, and setting you up for an active and profitable career.

Does that sound like something that would interest you?

If so, read on. Let's explore how you can audition for your career, not the job.

 Notes

----

PART ONE

SHERLOCK HOLMESING THE TEXT®

Sanford Meisner's definition of acting on stage:
"Living truthfully within a given set of imaginary circumstances."

Tim Phillip's definition of acting for the camera:
"Being human in human circumstances."

One of the reasons this book exists is to make auditioning fun. It is possible to maintain or regain the enthusiasm that inspired you to act and drew you into the profession in the first place. The methods in this book are for professional actors who are dedicated to enjoying their work, even if that work is five minutes that occur during an audition.

As an actor, you rely upon producers of films and television programs for your livelihood. There's a definite sense that they have power and you do not. But if you get caught up in this kind of thinking and the politics of the profession, if you perceive yourself as an outsider trying to break in, this can make you feel tense and resentful, and interfere with your self-expression. It's necessary to understand the traps of certain mindsets, and take control of your life by being in charge of your thought processes.

So part of your task as an actor is *making your job fun.* After all, isn't that the real reason you started acting in the first place? Not because you thought you would make money at it, not for retirement benefits, not for job security? If those things were more important to you than the creative exploration of your psychological makeup and telling stories that have the power to move people to laughter and tears, it's likely you would go and get a steady job (a "real" job?) in a different profession. Having fun as an actor means you impact people's lives in a meaningful way, starting with your own.

This book is not really for beginning actors, except perhaps in an aspirational way, because if you're a complete novice then you still need to go out and learn foundational skills, such as The Meisner Technique, in order for the advice in this book to be truly useful to you. I'm not going to stop and teach you how to generate a feeling, do inner parallels, or break scenes into actionable beats. All I'm going to do is tell you when these things are needed. It's your job to bring your skills and imagination to the work.

Everything begins with how you approach your work. This book teaches an approach to preparing for auditions on camera, which are different than auditions for the stage. For one thing, on stage you have to be bigger than life so that your thoughts and feelings can be read by individuals who are seated far away in the back of the room. On stage people are watching actions. On camera they're watching thoughts. Yes, thoughts and behavior need to be authentic on stage, however there are specific techniques for vocal projection and movement through the three-dimensional space of a theatre that are distinct. Film acting is more intimate. It can be like standing in a phone booth with your scene partner pressed against you while having a camera shoved up your nose. You don't have to project your voice because the microphone can hear a whisper. And every subtle, fleeting thought you have that flickers behind your eyes is captured precisely.

The camera never flinches. It never lies. *It reveals knowledge.*

The reality of the on-camera audition room is that you won't be moving around much. You'll sit in a chair across from an off-screen reader (sometimes an actor, but just as often a casting director or an assistant) with a digital camera aimed at you. The camera operator will set the frame of the shot medium-close on your head and upper torso. If you're thinking, *I hope I look good. Oh no, what's my next line?* the camera will record those ideas, which relate to *your* circumstances, rather than the character's thoughts about the imaginary situation in which you're supposed to be immersed.

My goal is to teach you how to do homework on the meaning of the script so that you always have sufficient knowledge behind your eyes to be engaging on film and make a durable impression. We'll discuss how to become better at preparing a performance on the turn of a dime. This is a method that you can practice and, over time, master.

Make the Commitment to Master Your Craft

Remember, although acting is fun, rehearsing sometimes feels hard. Even so, you must rehearse if you want to move from the D-list to the C-list, from the C-list to the B-list, and possibly even make it to the A-list. For actors, talent is the ability to move into an imaginary world quickly and with relatively little effort. You are either born with this talent or you are not. Those of us who aren't as naturally gifted learn to craft our roles so we may compete with more talented actors. Talent of any degree can be enhanced with crafting. Crafting, which takes place during the rehearsal process, levels the playing field. Of course, crafting helps even the best actors make specific, appropriate choices.

Take a lesson from Larry Bird, the Hall of Fame basketball player for the Boston Celtics, who ESPN ranks as one of the fifty greatest athletes of the twentieth century. Bird was at the peak of his game in the '80s at the same time that Magic Johnson played for the Los Angeles Lakers. Johnson had a natural talent. Bird had to work for it. He would do free throws on his own for two hours before and after team practices. His commitment to developing his talent made him a competitor to be reckoned with. I want you to be as disciplined in practicing your skills so you're ready to play the game.

There isn't a miraculous potion you can take to be a good actor. It takes time and commitment to master the craft. But the tools do work if you practice them diligently. You may not want to believe it, but even the actors you most admire craft their butts off so that their talent will be there for them when they need it. They don't walk on set and wing it. Their crafting has to be there already. One of the best actors of our age, Anthony Hopkins (*The Silence of the Lambs, Remains of the Day*), for example, has an extremely thorough way of working. He reportedly reads the scripts of the films he does 250 times. During those readings, he finds the life in what he is saying and doing. He doesn't supply it; he discovers it in the script. Then, he crafts.

Before you can do what Hopkins does that gets him superb results, you will have to learn how to read a script properly.

"I know how to read!" you may protest.

No, you don't—at least not the way I'm talking about. You probably did as a child, but if you're like the thousands of film and television actors I've coached and taught over the years, you usually read for results rather than for the absorption of information. Few of us, as adults with busy lives, give ourselves permission and time to read, wonder, and daydream like little kids. Instead, we shoot for results and we're in a big hurry to attain those results immediately. Now I'm asking you to become more sponge like.

Pay attention. There is a risk in working the way I'm suggesting. To succeed as an actor in film and television, you have to be willing to risk being the world's most boring, do-nothing actor. The camera doesn't see "acting." It sees knowledge. You have to be willing to trust that the camera will see what you know after reading the script. And you have to read the script in a certain way if you want to *know* anything that's actable.

Becoming a Good Detective

Emmy Award-winning actor Richard Schiff, a former student of mine whom I have also coached on occasion, called me up about twelve years ago when he was working on a project with Al Pacino. This was before Richard was cast in *The West Wing* television series, in the role of Toby Ziegler for which he won his Emmy. After a table reading, he told me, "Now I understand what you meant! Pacino doesn't supply *anything*," meaning that Pacino did nothing on a line during that early group reading (except to say the words out loud) until he found a logical reason to do it. By the time that film was made, I'm sure Pacino had made plenty of super-specific choices. He just didn't push ahead of himself to get to some preconceived results. He was willing to thoroughly read and analyze the script before crafting his performance.

Performing for an audition is different from performing once you have been hired for a role in a film or a television production in that there is much less rehearsal time. When your agent or manager, or a casting director provides you with the sides for an audition, you may have these few pages from the script overnight or you may only have them for fifteen to twenty minutes. In either case, normally you won't have much to go on. When I was an actor, I used to sit in the reception area of the audition working with my script. Sometimes I'd wave other actors to go on ahead of me. They thought I was being a nice guy, but really I was being shrewd. I was using those extra minutes of precious time to make discoveries. I was *Sherlock Holmesing* my script.

To get a handle on a role, you must use curiosity, intuition, and deductive reasoning to approach the script. In the chapters of Part One, we'll consider how these three tools can help you be successful in various phases of the process of rapid script analysis. You don't want to leap to assumptions about a character and a scene. It's important to keep an open mind and build a case for the character traits and behavior you're being asked to invent and portray using the factual evidence you pick up from the script line by line.

Let's take a moment to consider what these tools can do for you.

Get Curious

Curiosity means opening your mind to receive answers by asking questions. What's my name? Where am I? What happened before this scene took place? Asking those and as many other questions as you can think of is the foundation of your investigation. You are hunting for clues. Writers are clever at hiding clues in unexpected places. They write and rewrite scripts until all kinds of juicy tidbits of information are embedded in them. But they try not to squeeze all the juice into the dialogue on the first page; preferring for dramatic reasons to let the juice trickle out as a scene develops over several pages. Every clue you discover represents a potential acting choice for you ultimately to make.

The dictionary definition of curiosity is "the desire to find out or know things." And what makes things curious, or interesting, to know is that they are rare or unusual. They stand out in some way from the background. As you cultivate your curiosity, that's what you are looking for, too. What stands out as noteworthy? Why were these words chosen and not others? When Arthur Conan Doyle's exceptional detective, Sherlock Holmes, got interested in a case, he used to say to his friend Dr. Watson, "The game is afoot!" Then they'd go off hunting with magnifying glasses and rulers, and leaving no stone unturned. No detail was dismissed by Holmes as so small and unremarkable that it could be ignored. They knew that in the end a seemingly insignificant detail might solve their puzzle.

In scripts, there are *never* any insignificant details. Sniff out those clues.

Intuition

Intuition, according to the *Oxford American Dictionary*, is the "power of knowing or understanding something immediately without reasoning or being taught." Where does intuition come from? It's a form of innate intelligence that everyone has that's somehow hardwired into the body. It's the ability to make a cognitive leap or form an insight based on slender evidence, and at the same time to *sense* and *feel* the rightness of it.

Often when I am teaching my workshops, as soon as I start talking about intuition I see all the women in the room nodding their heads and the men furrowing their brows. Women get this because they are acculturated to trust their feelings. Nonetheless, men share this ability. Call it gut instinct. Call it whatever you like. If you practice listening to the inner voice that chimes up to tell you what more might be true for a character in a script you are reading, you will begin to discover additional avenues of behavior to play.

Since you'll often be preparing for an audition in a relatively short time span, viewing your intuitive hunches as valuable clues can enrich your interpretation of a script.

If you're familiar with the tales of Sherlock Holmes, you'll no doubt recall that upon occasion he would lock himself away in his apartment, where he would play his violin for hours on end, letting his mind wander freely this way and that while reflecting upon his cases. I believe at such times he was allowing his intuition to speak to him. When he re-emerged, he would generally continue in the hot pursuit of his suspect.

Divergent thinking, the aspect of the creative process whereby we are allowing more possibilities and options to be made available to us, involves the use of the intuition. It's not something forced. It's something that naturally emerges out of our curiosity and questioning. Taking place before we pin ourselves down and make firm choices, the insights that come from daydreaming and *sensing what could be,* are byproducts of all that we have seen, heard, smelled, tasted, touched, and experienced throughout our lifetimes flashing back into our awareness spontaneously when we need them.

If you make room for intuitive hits to come to mind while you are reading a script, you may find that you know more about the human being you are being asked to become than the actual words on the page express. You might just *guess at* something deeper that you can use to color the acting choices you ultimately make. Also, once you indulge your *suspicions* you may find that there are lines that actually support your intuition.

Deductive Reasoning

If intuition is a spontaneous experience of immediate insight, deduction is its rational counterpart and, therefore, slightly slower to provide answers. It's almost mathematical. Meaning that as you read your sides you are adding up the discoveries you make until you are certain about the facts that are being set out before you. If one plus one equals two, then two minus one surely must equal one. Similarly, if you add up all the clues you uncover and combine this evidence with the evidence of the information provided to you in the character breakdown, then certain conclusions can be drawn.

The trick in preparing an audition is not to jump to conclusions because you want to reach a specific result. Dramatic writing, if it's skillful, has twists and turns in it. Often a character has a past history that motivates action, but is not discussed directly in dialogue. It has been said that in a tightly-written script there is only one choice a character could make in a given scene based upon who that person has demonstrated being and the circumstances in which the character is immersed. That's a workable definition. If in one scene a script reveals that a character is a "good mother," it would be out of character for her to behave irresponsibly towards her children... unless new circumstances dictate she does so. What makes a scene dramatic is when a human being is being pushed in some direction—and then we watch to see how it is resolved.

As an actor, you need to serve the script and embrace the given circumstances. Your job is to deduce these, testing your initial assumptions and guesswork against the script, and logically reason both *what* your character knows and *when* the character knows it. Since you have to play a scene line by line, beat by beat, part of what you are doing is learning to follow the path of events and the path of thoughts in every scene as your character experiences them.

Sherlock Holmes was a master logician. Always my favorite aspect of the stories about him has been how he could meet unfamiliar people and with a short glance at their appearance deduce very specific facts about their lives and recent activities. He had an uncanny ability to apprehend details that went far beyond what ordinary people could see with their untrained eyes, because they didn't know what mattered. This ability made him seem supernaturally intelligent and gave him an advantage in his profession. By comparison, the police were like bumbling fools who were constantly misdirected.

As an actor, as you practice looking with curiosity for clues about what matters in the different sides you are given, like Holmes you will gain an advantage over your peers. You will learn to reason how these clues add up, and why they matter, and this will enable you to make strong, bold acting choices that you can rely upon to show up on film when a camera is pointed at you. You'll become interesting to watch since you'll always have something happening behind your eyes. And you'll be more responsive and real, and less forced, because when you know what you know, it's just there; you won't have to fake it to demonstrate it. Some of the most powerful scene work I've observed is presented in great stillness. The energy is all in the eyes and the voice, and its riveting to watch it on screen.

The Game Is Afoot

So let's get to it. Let's look at all those compelling questions that are part of this creative rapid script analysis process. At first, you may feel a little awkward using it. Given practice, however, you'll be able to do this faster and with more confidence. Remember, that this is how you can level the playing field and have more fun.

 Notes

----

CHAPTER 1
WHAT'S THE PROJECT CALLED?

> *The job of the dramatist is to make the audience wonder what happens next."*
> **—David Mamet**

Agents, managers, and casting directors tend to talk fast, as they are busy people (or perhaps because they wish to seem so). The point being, it's up to you to stand up for yourself and ask for what you need from them if you don't get it. Upon learning about an upcoming audition, there are three things you must be sure to receive:

- *The sides:* one or more scenes from the script that you will read during the audition.

- *The character breakdown:* a description of your character.

- *The exact date, time, and location of the audition:* you don't want to miss the audition, to get lost and show up late, or to feel anxious about any logistical details.

- *The name of the casting director, writer/producer, and director:* You want to know who you're dealing with, both so you can schmooze effortlessly with the creative team if you need to, and also so you can review their past projects and get a sense of their style.

Once you have these few necessities in hand, your Sherlock Holmesing can begin.

Your First Acting Clue

The first acting clue—the title of the project—is so obvious that it would be easy to overlook. But don't make the mistake of taking anything for granted. Leave no stone unturned. Remember, as you hold your script in hand and read through it for the first time, your aim should be to find any and all actable information in it. You will use curiosity, intuition, and deductive reasoning. The screenwriter is speaking to you in a code, a cryptic message that you must crack.

Talk aloud to yourself as you go along. Ask questions. Say to yourself: "I think that…, "I feel that…," "I'm guessing that…," "It seems possible that . . .," and "I wonder if…" Never forget that you are a detective solving a crime.

The crime, in this case, is your role. The sides are the evidence.

Deduction is how you put all the clues together at the end. That is when you make choices and use your craft as an actor. But you can't deduce correctly until you gather all of the evidence.

Keep a pencil handy (with a good eraser) and jot down notes in the margin of your sides as you go along. You might also write down your suspicions and impressions about the character and the scenes in a special notebook reserved for this purpose.

As you read the title for the very first time, pause and reflect. *What could this mean? What could it tell me about who my character is? Or about the scene I've been handed?*

The Definition of a Scene

A scene is a compression of time, space, and reality. Compression requires that everything which takes place in a scene is non-ordinary or heightened reality. Every word and every symbol you see in your script matters because the writer has to communicate so much in such a short span of time. Every comma, every ellipses, every parenthetical description was specifically chosen by the screenwriter to help you move the plot and relationships forward. Do not miss a single thing!

It is beneficial for actors to understand how screenwriters think, as the elements of their craft directly impact ours. We are looking for the life that exists behind and between the lines, as much as on the lines.

In 2005, the renowned playwright and director David Mamet wrote a memo to the staff writers of *The Unit,* a then-new television action series he created and executive produced about the men of a Special Forces unit and their wives. Leaked on the Internet, this memo has been widely circulated among screenwriters because of its theme: What makes good television? In essence, it addresses the reason for compression. As he says, "We are tasked with, it seems, cramming a shitload of *information* into a little bit of time... But note: the audience will not tune in to watch information.... The audience will only tune in and stay tuned to watch drama."[1]

As an actor, you must always serve the writer's intentions. You must say the lines you are given and make sense of them whether they are poorly or well written, and even if they represent nothing more than story exposition. This means that some lines report facts with no inherent drama in them, background details that *must* be communicated for the story to make sense to the audience. A skillful writer finds entertaining ways to dramatize exposition, incorporating facts into scenes that advance the plot or reveal something about the character. But sometimes you will just have to spit out expository lines and do your best to make a moment truthful despite dull, or even stupid, writing.

Mamet defines drama as "the quest of the hero to overcome those things which prevent him from achieving a specific, *acute* goal." He advises: "We, the writers, must ask ourselves of every scene these three questions: 1) Who wants what? 2) What happens if the hero doesn't get it? 3) Why now? The answers to these questions are litmus paper."[2] As an actor, you need to be looking for the answers that the writer has hopefully provided you to these questions. It is not your job to supply the answers, but to truthfully embody the answers the writer has found in a human way.

Later in his memo Mamet continues, "Remember you are writing for a visual medium. *Most* television writing, ours included, sounds like *radio*. The *camera* can do the explaining for you. *Let* it. What are the characters *doing* 'literally'? What are they handling, what are they reading? What are they watching on television, what are they *seeing?* If you pretend the characters can't speak, and write a silent movie, you will be writing great drama."[3]

In an audition, you won't actually be doing anything physical. You'll either sit or you will stand. In rare instances, you might go from standing to seated or seated to standing.

But you won't be moving around the room. An audition really is a close-up. Nonetheless, you need to know, in explicit detail, what your character will be doing when it comes time to shoot the scene for real. Know this and the camera will see it behind your eyes.

To test this principle, lower the volume on your television and study the performances of the actors in your favorite programs. See what happens during their close-ups. A good program to use for this particular exploration is *The Good Wife,* starring Julianna Margulies, as the camerawork in every scene of this show includes many close-ups.

Watch Kyra Sedgwick eating in *The Closer.* You know exactly how she feels and what she thinks about every piece of cake or Ding Dong she consumes, even though she doesn't ever talk about it. Sedgwick's knowledge is revealed by her transparency.

Due to the compressed nature of a scene, writers hide clues to meaning everywhere. The script is encoded material that is a metaphor for life—not life itself. The average one-hour episode of a TV show encompasses forty-eight pages of script. A half-hour episode is written in twenty-four pages. A two-hour film averages 120 scripted pages.

Where to begin decoding this mystery that is your script? Right where the audience begins: with the title of the project.

The First Question: What Does the Title of the Show/Film Tell Me?

Consider the titles of several popular television series and what they can tell us at a glance. Feel free to come up with your own impressions. This is purely intuitive.

Cougar Town: middle-aged women hungry for sex—possibly with younger men—probably funny.

Rookie Blue: novice cops in uniform, possibly with "the blues."

Private Practice: the intimate lives of doctors in a practice together—probably a primetime soap opera.

Desperate Housewives: women living in houses who are unhappy—probably funny.

Modern Family: family escapades—possibly nontraditional family combinations—probably funny.

Criminal Minds: a crime drama where police "profilers" chase bad guys and solve cases based on thinking like the criminals.

Scoundrels: criminals up to mischief—probably funny.

No Ordinary Family: a family with something special about its members. (Further investigation leads us to know the special thing is having super powers like comic book heroes.)

My Generation: a look at people of the same age—probably relatively young people, maybe Gen X people.

The Big Bang Theory: featuring scientists—possibly tongue-in-cheek funny.

Hawaii Five-O: remake of a classic program, set in Hawaii, featuring cops.

The Defenders: featuring lawyers who work for criminals. Not sure, could be funny.

Burn Notice: don't know offhand, sounds official—sounds *hot.*

Californication: sex in California—probably funny. And it sounds perverse or intellectual.

Stargate Universe: science fiction, spinoff of an earlier program, involving a gate to the stars (whatever that is) and the entire universe (or "a" universe, and is it ours?).

Use your curiosity and speak aloud to yourself. Literally ask, "What could this title mean?" At this stage, with a new project, you won't have much else to go on.

Here's how Sherlock Holmesing works in practice. Let's take *CSI,* as an example. What do those initials stand for? The answer: crime scene investigators. Intuitively we'd surely guess this program was about forensic scientists, the investigators who solve crimes, and it is possibly gritty. If we had seen any of the earlier three versions of the show, we'd also know it was stylish, set in Las Vegas, Miami, or Los Angeles.

You would also wonder, wouldn't you, who this insight makes your character. Are you perhaps a victim, a criminal, a witness, an informant, or a crime solver? How does your character serve the plot of the episode (or ongoing series of episodes) for which you are being asked to audition? Knowing the structure of a one-hour crime drama, you can logically surmise that each episode covers the commission, investigation, and solving of a significant crime. Looking at the title opens your mind to receive guidance from the script about how to handle the material.

Television Episode Titles

Beyond the title of the show, when you are shooting a television series, every episode has its own title. This is another clue to the central focus of that episode's investigation. From *CSI: NY* come episode titles like "Pay Up," "Hostage," "Cold Reveal," "Personal Foul," and "Admissions." What intuitive hunch do you get from any of these? They seem to be rather terse phrases. Are they plays on words (puns) or literal descriptions of the episode plots? We don't know yet.

Ask, what could that last episode title mean… *admissions?* An "admission" is a revelation of something personal and often embarrassing, like an admission of an error or a failing—or of guilt. When you look at the breakdown for this episode, you might learn that it involves a guidance counselor in a high school advising students about the college admissions process. There may be a double entendre here (most likely there is) about college admissions and guilty admissions.

Let your curiosity lead you to ask questions that result from your hunches. Put them in the background of your mind as open questions that may yield useful knowledge as you read further down the page and begin to make decisions. If you've been given a pivotal scene to prepare, such as the scene where your character makes a confession to the police, having a point of view derived from the episode title could help you craft an interesting performance or moment.

At the top of your sides, instead of an episode title, you might also see the letters T.B.D. These stand for "to be determined." This indicates that the script is still a work in progress. As it hasn't been finalized, your work will be in vain if you memorize it now since the screenwriter hasn't yet entirely solved the puzzle of the program. This is a sign to be as mentally nimble as you can be. Don't worry though; you won't be dealing with last-minute rewrites during a five- or ten-minute audition.

Film Titles

Like the names of television series, the name of a film should express that which is most central about it. A film title is basically code for the most important element of the plot, the context, or a lead character. Think back and you'll probably remember some titles of movies, for instance (in chronological order): *Sophie's Choice; Good Morning, Vietnam; Do the Right Thing; Catch Me If You Can;* and *The Motorcycle Diaries.*

Do an intuition test on the title of any film you have admired to see whether it aptly communicates the essence of the movie. While a retrospective inquiry, this practice session should reinforce the point of how much you can learn about a project from its title. Remember that normally at this stage you haven't read the sides yet. You are just beginning to open up a process of inquiry. This is what you'd discover in looking back.

Sophie's Choice (1982) with a script by Alan J. Pakula adapted from a novel by William Styron, starred Meryl Streep as a post-World War Two Polish immigrant living in New York City, a Nazi concentration camp survivor who, as we learn towards the end of the film, was forced to make a terrible choice to save either her son or her daughter from being murdered. Her choice is a central mystery that informs the character, a woman who enthralls the young, male protagonist nicknamed Stingo.

If you were auditioning for this film, knowing your character's relationship to Sophie or how your character factors into the story of her making her choice or what she does afterwards might be a clue to how to craft your performance.

Good Morning, Vietnam (1987), with a script by Mitch Markowitz, starred Robin Williams as an irreverent disk jockey assigned to the U.S. Armed Services Radio station in Hanoi, Vietnam, during the war. Every morning the character begins his program with the cheerful phrase, "Good morning, Vietnam!" His mandated role as a morale booster for the soldiers and his on-air comments during his tour of duty change as the tide of the war turns against the U.S. and as the morality of what the American troops are doing is called into question. The title not only refers to the literal wakeup call the program serves as every morning for the soldiers, but it signifies the character's wakeup call to what is happening around him and America's wakeup call to a "bad war."

If you were auditioning for this film, the title might give you an actable clue in regard to the Vietnam War era. Does your audition scene take place before, during, or after an awakening?

Do the Right Thing (1989), written and directed by Spike Lee, as well as starring him, is a film about bigotry and racial hatred that erupt in an urban neighborhood on a sweltering summer day. It's an ironic title, because the film is ambivalent about what the "right thing to do" is. As an advisory, it keeps the audience wondering whose point of view to embrace. "Rightness" is subjective.

If you were auditioning for this film, you might do well to get curious about your character's racial attitudes. Is the title a clue to develop a point of view about "righteous" behavior?

Catch Me If You Can (2002), with a script by Jeff Nathanson adapted from a book by Frank Abagnale, Jr., and Stan Redding, starred Leonardo DiCaprio and Tom Hanks, who respectively play a con artist and the federal agent trying to arrest him. If you were auditioning for this film, how might the title inform your character's behavior? Wouldn't you be curious about where your character interacts either with the pursuer or the pursued? It's a lighthearted title. Why?

The Motorcycle Diaries (2004), a Latin American film scripted by Jose Rivera, adapted from both Ernesto "Che" Guevara's actual diaries and a book about his youth by Alberto Granado, focuses on a road trip across South America—by motorcycle—that took place when the world-famous Latin activist/rebel, a hero to many people, was taking time off from studying to be a doctor. Was it this journey that caused him to find his life's purpose of helping oppressed people? What personality traits developed out of this temporary experience of poverty and hardship? Knowing the significance of this title could hold a clue for an actor auditioning for the project.

Always ask questions and make guesses about the title. Be curious. Heed your intuition.

Researching Past Episodes and Precursors

When you read the script for a television show, at the top of the page, there is always a number. Let's say, 303. This particular number means you're looking at sides from the script of the third episode in the third season. Script numbering is similar to hotel room or office suite numbering, except that script numbers begin with the number of the season instead of the floor.

The third season is a great season to be on a particular show. You know it is a hit! It's been renewed twice, kept on the air by the studio executives. It's earning money for the advertisers because it's getting good ratings.

If you see the number 703, then you can guess the show is soon to be cancelled. After all, it has been on the air for seven seasons already. The regular characters are thoroughly developed. The style of the program is probably locked into place. It is a brand-name product with a devoted following that knows the specific commodity to expect every week.

If you see 103, then you know it is the show's first season and you really don't know if it's going to do well. The kinks may not have been worked out yet. The characters are new. Their histories, personalities, and relationships haven't been developed much by the writers.

By taking the time to view some past episodes of an ongoing series before your audition you can get a sense of the storytelling style that might ultimately help you. If it's a gritty crime drama, that's one style. If it's a situation comedy, that's another. If you know the show you are trying out for, you can learn the style of the show ahead of time. Entering the audition room with sensitivity for the material to which you have to pay homage means the producer doesn't have to educate you. This could be a favorable factor leaning toward your selection.

One student of mine auditioned for an episode of *Gilmore Girls,* a show whose dialogue was often witty banter delivered rapid-fire. The pace was generally so quick, in fact, that scripts for *Gilmore Girls* usually ran to sixty pages instead of the customary forty-eight. When the producer heard my student read his scene in style, he thanked him for doing it that way and then gave him the job on the spot—all because he understood the way the show was paced.

In addition to watching earlier episodes of a running program, other precursors that you might want to investigate online include the movies that shows are based upon. For instance, if you had an audition for a part in the TV show

Nikita, you could view the French film *La Femme Nikita* (1990) or its American remake, *The Point of No Return* (1993). You wouldn't want to make everything you did in your audition an imitation of those films; think of it as just another way to establish an intuitive sense of the concept and approach based on the title.

You can stream full episodes of currently airing TV shows (often including episodes from past seasons) on the websites of the various broadcast networks (NBC.com, CBS.com, Fox.com, ABC.com, and so forth) or stream reruns of older programs on websites like Hulu.com. You can either stream movies or view them on DVD by mail order from companies like Netflix.com, or watch them on a pay-per-view channel.

What if the project you're auditioning for is a spinoff of a popular show? A classic example of a spinoff is the program *Frasier*, starring Kelsey Grammer, which was a very successful sequel to *Cheers*. Knowing the history of the leading character, as drawn from the original program where he was not the main character, may help you understand how to relate to this character in the new context. Here, among other traits, you would discover that the character of Dr. Frasier Crane is a psychiatrist who often brags about his intelligence and his taste for the finer things in life. That made him different than the main character of Sam Malone, the former pro-baseball player in *Cheers*; and it also made him the opposite of his blue-collar father, a retired policeman, who is one of his foils in *Frasier*. There's a lot of information available to you from simple research.

Use everything you discover from the project title for inspiration in your crafting process. In the end, your knowledge will help you make clear, specific, interesting, and appropriate choices for your on-camera audition.

Notes

CHAPTER 2
WHAT'S MY NAME?

❝ *The creative mind plays with objects it loves.*"
—**Carl Gustav Jung**

One of the greatest influences on my acting is Academy Award-winner Robert Duvall, who has enjoyed a long and distinguished career in film and television, as well as on stage, winning and being nominated for many prestigious awards for his work in films such as *Tender Mercies*, *The Apostle* (which he also wrote and directed), *A Civil Action, Rambling Rose, The Great Santini, Apocalypse Now,* and *The Godfather,* and in the TV mini-series *Broken Trail.* We became friends and he cast me in a project he was directing called *Angelo My Love,* which was released in 1983, the same year he won his Best Actor Oscar. Subsequently, we acted together in a less memorable picture called *The Lightship.* Our friendship gave me the opportunity to observe his work habits up close.

Years ago, I remember sitting alone in the kitchen at Duvall's farmhouse in Virginia, drinking a beer. Our wives had gone out, and he and I were alone in the house. I could hear him talking aloud in another part of the house, so I peeked around the doorframe to see what he was doing. He was seated in a formal dining room chair with a script on his lap, and he was talking to it. Every once in a while he would smack the paper with the back of his hand.

Robert caught me watching him and said, "Timmy, look here! Look who I have a chance to be!"

It still gives me goose bumps when I think about it. What a healthy way to begin working on a script. I hope that's why you started acting, too: because you wanted to portray other people, to experience being human under imaginary circumstances.

Always pick up your script to see who you get a chance to be, not "who 'they' want me to be so I can get this job." You simply can't act according to your guess about someone else's expectations. Yes, you have to hit the right moments in the script. You have to tease out all the information that the screenwriter has provided and reveal it in your audition. But you're not a mind reader and, more importantly, you will be hired—if you are—for the specific qualities that you possess and how the life of the character moves through your body. As Duvall terms it, as an actor you *bend* yourself to own the character in a specific moment. You remain you; you're not actually becoming someone else. If you were this character, living in this situation, what would that *be* like?

My endeavor, especially in the world of film and television, is to bring actors back down to the level of being human during an audition. Curiosity about who you get to be for a few minutes is the only reason to pick up the sides—not because you need the money. We all know you need money. You're just like the thousands of other actors who are competing for the same on-camera parts in the major markets like

Los Angeles, New York, and Chicago. They're auditioning for roles in blockbuster studio films, independent films, and television series, as well as commercials, animated or semi-animated films, and the new vehicle of the Internet television productions. If you are more caught up in your desire for employment than in your curiosity about your character, it will be evident in your audition. You must find a way to shift your attention to *who you are being.*

The Character Breakdown

Go to the breakdown first. The breakdown is helpful in that it gives you a general overview of your character: a name, an age, an occupation, and elements of personality that the producers feel are relevant to the performance they want to see. Depending on the size of the role there will be more or less to glean from the breakdown. It could say as little as "a uniform cop" or "a nurse," and not include a name. It could also say things that seem contradictory, such as "tough, but gentle." My recommendation is that you read the breakdown with curiosity and intuition, preparing to test your guesses against the scene or scenes you've been given to read. Understand that it is merely describing different qualities of the character that will be revealed somewhere in the script. It is your responsibility to find appropriate moments in the script where the different qualities of your character that are named in the breakdown could reveal themselves. At this stage, you are seeking opportunities to demonstrate many possible aspects of character.

You should not necessarily try to cram all of those qualities into the same scene, and *definitely* do not try to display them all on the same line. If you put "tough" and "gentle" together they will cancel each other out. Alternating qualities can be interesting, if the script requires it. In a given scene there may be one place for you to show gentleness, and then another place for toughness. But in that one scene there may only be room for toughness. In a different scene found later in the script, there is only gentleness. The point being, as an actor you can only play one dimension of a character in any given moment.

At this point in your preparation for your audition, it is too soon to craft moments. Crafting must always follow thorough investigation. Don't jump ahead of yourself.

The first question to ask about your character is "What's my name?" The writer carefully chose this name for the character and it is a critical clue in the process of discovering who you get to be. With time and practice, you'll do this instinctively.

Let's take a look at the two leading characters in the television series *The Good Guys,* as an example of how to Sherlock Holmes a name. In a simple breakdown for the show, Dan Stark (played by Bradley Whitford) is described as a "washed-up detective." Jack Bailey (played by Colin Hanks) is described as a "young, by-the-book detective." We also learn that they are partners in the "property crimes division." One is at the end of his career and one is at the beginning. Already, from only this simple set of information, we can intuit a tremendous amount about the personalities of these two men—the eponymous "good guys" of this program—and the possible dynamic that exists between them. Getting curious, we explore further.

From the title of the show, *The Good Guys,* and the breakdown, we know that it's about cops, and it's likely to involve tongue-in-cheek comedy because it's an ironic title, clearly not meant to be taken at face value. What does it mean to solve cases involving property crimes? A crime against property means theft. When little boys play cops and robbers, aren't the good guys always the cops and the "bad guys" the criminals? Might this therefore be a show about cops who act like little boys? Or who are treated like little boys? Do they take their job seriously? Or do they want to be taken more seriously as professionals? Intuitively, we can guess this is an issue for them as detectives.

Also, from the title the very idea of "good" is being called into question. Are our leading characters good or bad as detectives? Maybe they are corrupt or incompetent? We don't know yet. Ultimately, the script will tell us. Let's keep looking for clues.

Dan is an abbreviation of Daniel. It has a manly ring to it. Short, as if there's not a lot to be said. Maybe he talks little—perhaps in monosyllables? Maybe he's a tough guy? Yet, Dan also sounds kind of friendly. Isn't this the name of someone you might like to grab a beer with? But what about his full name, Daniel? Wasn't Daniel the guy from the Bible who walked into the lion's den? Does this guy walk directly into danger and come out unharmed?

Remember, we don't have answers yet; here we're just forming hunches.

Dan's surname is Stark. In turning to the dictionary, we find the definitions: "barren, empty, cheerless, desolate, and lifeless." For further consideration, there's also the phrase "stark raving mad." What combination of these qualities might Dan Stark possess? Later, when you're crafting the part you might look for places to include a little bit of lunacy, a little bit of emptiness, toughness, boyishness, and so forth—if the script confirms it.

What about the name Jack Bailey? Who might our other "good guy" be? Jack of all trades? Jack be nimble, Jack be quick, Jack jumped over the candlestick? Jack and the Beanstalk? Jack the Ripper? It's a comedy and he's "good," so our Jack is probably not evil—but we'll find out the truth in the script. For now, we're being intuitive.

What other associations come up with the name Jack? Jack is a nickname for John, your regular or average man, an unidentified man: John Doe. It's conventional. Normal. There is no hint of lunacy in it. This take seems to be confirmed by the breakdown, where it says he goes "by-the-book." His approach as a detective could be antithetical to Dan's, a potential source of conflict between them. Conflict is a key ingredient in drama. But he's not called John; he's called Jack, which implies a kind of informality. Maybe there's something in that idea? Of course, it has a straightforward ring to it, directness. A jack is a tool you use to change a spare tire. It is a lever. It's how you get the heavy lifting done.

Jack's surname is Bailey. What does our intuition tell us about this name? Bailing water out of a leaky boat? Bailing a friend out of trouble? The name Bailey is also reminiscent to me of the character, George Bailey (played by Jimmy Stewart), from the classic Christmas film *It's a Wonderful Life* by Frank Capra. That's a sentimental favorite. That Bailey was a likeable fellow, a friend to everybody in his town, a decent father and husband, a decent human being. Might our Jack also be decent?

As an aside, the angel in Capra's film was called Clarence Oddbody. Right? Get it? In that film, Clarence—a peculiar character—was trying to do a good deed to get his wings. I wonder if Dan Stark is Jack's Oddbody, his angel trying to prove himself? *Hmm.*

These are the kind of questions and guesses you should be making with the name of the character you are being asked to be and the name of the TV program or film. This is what you will do from now on before you even read any specific lines from the script.

Notes

intuition becomes very
elaborate

CHAPTER 3
WHERE AM I?

> *An actor must interpret life, and in order to do so must be willing to accept all experiences that life has to offer."*
> **—Marlon Brando**

The clinical definition of psychosis is not to know where you are, who you are, or what you are doing there. Unless the character you are being asked to portray is supposed to be insane or to have amnesia, those pieces of information are important for you, the actor, to ascertain or decide, as these are items your character *without question* would know.

That being said, you can be intuitive about the location, for although the script is likely to tell you where you are, knowledge is experiential rather than remembered.

When I lecture on "Sherlock Holmesing the Text®," I usually hand out a writer's draft of a scene from *CSI: NY,* which is a spinoff of the original *CSI.* There are three shows in this CBS-TV franchise. *CSI,* set in Las Vegas, which, until 2009, starred William Petersen as the head of the forensic science unit of the police department, at which point he was replaced by a new character played by Laurence Fishburne (nominated for an Oscar for his role as Ike Turner in *What's Love Got to Do with It,* but perhaps best known for playing Morpheus in *The Matrix*). The sequel to that was *CSI: Miami,* which starred David Caruso, originally of *NYPD Blue* fame. The second spinoff, *CSI: NY,* stars Gary Sinese (nominated for an Academy Award for his role in *Forrest Gump*) as Detective Mckenna "Mac" Taylor and Melina Kanakaredes (who has since left the shows) as his partner Detective Stella Bonasera.

At the start of the scene from *CSI: NY* that we're investigating, all we know is that the script picks up with a scene in a kitchen, where someone is in the process of photographing vegetable dishes. The script tells us that the kitchen counter is arranged with backdrops, a camera with a "macro lens," lights, and other equipment. A character named Sharon has the first line of dialogue: "I'm sorry—you caught me at work." This factoid is a helping hand offered to you by the screenwriter. And as Sanford Meisner used to say, "Every little moment has a meaning all its own." Once you deduce where Sharon is, also try to understand what it means to her to be in this location during this scene. It mainly means she is a photographer and has photographic equipment available to her.

The next line of dialogue in this particular scene is delivered by Mac, the character played by Gary Sinese. Mac says: "We won't take much of your time."

Given that this place is where Sharon works, and that Mac and Stella have just arrived, wouldn't you intuit that there is something missing from the beginning of this scene? An introduction! Clearly, Mac, Stella, and Sharon already know one another. Otherwise he would have said, "My name is Mac." Evidently, Sharon is expecting them, because she doesn't ask for their names or send them away. They may or may not have met before in person; it's possible they have only spoken on the telephone. Either way, Sharon is not surprised that the detectives have arrived in her workplace.

Do you see how valuable a single line can be? This one tiny exchange produced a clue that would be vital for your crafting process. Rest assured, however, that there is probably more to be discovered about the matter of where you are. As with every other choice the writer makes, there is nothing arbitrary about the environment in which a scene occurs. A little later in the scene we learn that this place is also Sharon's studio apartment. We are shown that it holds wheelchair ramps leading from room to room. We don't immediately know the ramps' relevance to the plot, but we should flag it for inquiry.

Always remember, casting is a process of elimination. The producers are narrowing down the field of candidates from many actors to the one actor they want. The actors who don't figure out which lines matter, and why, are easily and swiftly eliminated. The rest of the actors continue being allowed to compete.

Where you are directly influences your behavior. For comparison, consider how you would behave in a library, a church, a casino, a classroom, a courtroom, a sports arena, a candlelit restaurant, or a crowded bar. In film and television, your relationship to the place and to the other people in this place holds keys to your character's body language, speaking tones, and emotional reality. When you're crafting your performance, you'll circle back on the clues that you've picked up in the script and make specific choices that make your location personal to your character and evoke truthful life.

Staying curious about where you are as you Sherlock Holmes your sides may be the very question you need most to examine. You are building the body of knowledge that the camera will see behind your eyes in different moments of your performance. An interesting aspect of finding the clues is that pictures will pop into your head. People think and remember in pictures. Once you see a picture in your mind's eye, it becomes an experience, and experience becomes knowledge. Knowledge is what the camera sees.

The Many Facets of Where

The question of where you are is like a diamond with many facets. Your clue, which you will take directly from the script, could be a straightforward answer, like "on a boat." But it's more interesting if it's an elaborated answer, like "on a sinking boat" (*Titanic*), "on a boat being attacked by a shark" (*Jaws*), "on a party boat" (*Up in the Air*, remember the sequence of scenes in which the lead and his girlfriend crash a convention?), or "on a pirate ship" (*Pirates of the Caribbean*). Boat shmoat.

You want to know where you are because it may be relevant to the development of the plot—often it means something significant. How you say your lines will depend on what you know about where you are. Being at the top of a building is different if you're looking out at the view of the horizon versus looking down because you're getting ready to jump off it. Those are actable clues, answers to where you are.

Another facet of where you are is the quality of the environment around you. Is it an urban setting? Is it 2005 Chicago (*ER*) or 1920's Chicago, during the gangster-ridden era of Prohibition (*The Untouchables*)? Time and place are often linked. London is London. But London in the time of Henry the Eighth (*The Tudors*) can be distinguished from London during the German Blitzkrieg of 1940 in World War Two (*The End of the Affair*), which can be distinguished from London in 2001 (*Bridget Jones's Diary*). Is it a rural setting? A farm? A barbershop on Main Street in a small town? A back road winding through New Hampshire? Is it quiet, noisy, densely populated, or remote?

The flavor of ethnic cultures can be represented by where you are: San Francisco's Chinatown, New York's Little Italy, the very Irish Back Bay neighborhood of Boston, or a housing project occupied by generationally poor Blacks in Baltimore. Does your character reside in this setting, as one of its "natives," or is your character passing through? Does your character stand out like a sore thumb from the background?

Sometimes location can serve almost like another character in a project. For instance, Woody Allen's movie *Manhattan* (1979), Sydney Pollack's *Out of Africa* (1985), and the BBC/HBO series *Rome* (2005–2007), or William Wyler's *Roman Holiday* (1953), which stars Audrey Hepburn and Gregory Peck. Then there's *Breakfast at Tiffany's, Philadelphia Story, Detroit 1-8-7, Southland,* and *Californication.* Place holds information that will influence and color your choices when you are ready to craft.

- Who are you in relationship to this place?
- Why are you in this place?

- How did you get here?
- What are you doing here?
- What does this place look like, smell like, sound like, feel like?
- How do you feel about being in this place?

Make note of every detail in your script that has to do with where you are. If you see any mental pictures, make note of those, too.

Your character's location could be a place that is relevant to your character's profession, such as a shoe store, a laboratory, a hospital, a courtroom, or a strip club. But these days, with so many science fiction and fantasy projects being made, an answer to the question, "Where am I?" could be, "On a distant planet in a far away solar system."

Just as you did with the name of the project and the name of the character, once you discover the clues about your whereabouts, you need to intuit their meaning. Daydream aloud, "If this is where I am, then I suppose… I guess… I wonder if… I propose that…" As you continue reading line by line, verify your hunches against the remainder of the script. Never forget, the process of Sherlock Holmesing a script employs three key tools: curiosity, intuition, and deductive reasoning. Use these tools to absorb knowledge.

 Notes

----

 Notes

----

CHAPTER 4
WHAT HAS HAPPENED ALREADY?

> ❝❝ *Acting represents all that human beings experience, and if you want it to be 'nice,' you will never be a serious communicator of human experience."*
> **—Larry Moss**

Let's continue looking at the scene from *CSI: NY* that was introduced in the last chapter. Before we begin hunting for additional clues together, I'm going to let you in on the fact that this episode (season 3, episode 3) was ultimately titled "Love Run Cold" and its air date was October 4, 2006. The script was written by Timothy J. Lea. Along the top of the draft I give to my students, however, this information is not available. The title on my sides is only listed as "TBD."

The website TV.com offers a full plot description, including the following details of the murder scene: "Marathon runners race on the streets of New York. As they pass through Central Park, we see there's a detour, and soon we see the cause: a runner lies dead on the street. Mac says it looks like he fell and hit his head on the curb. Stella remarks that during a marathon, it would be easy to fall or be pushed and then get trampled, but their colleague Sheldon Hawkes suspects something else: brightness of the blood and lividity of the face seem to indicate cyanide poisoning. How is it possible in the middle of a marathon? Mac immediately suspects there's something wrong with the water being handed out at the aid station, and tells the workers to shut it down. The CSIs start picking up crushed water cups, and among them Stella finds a nozzle from a high pressure valve."[1]

In a second scene related to this investigation (there are two concurrent cases going on in this episode), which takes place in the morgue, the coroner tells Mac and Stella that the cause of death wasn't cyanide; it was actually carbon monoxide poisoning.

None of these facts would be known to you if you were auditioning from the sides I hand out; and yet they would be known to the characters Mac and Stella. Your job as an actor auditioning for the role of Sharon in this scene is to try to guess what has happened before the scene takes place. Again, you'll use curiosity, intuition, and deduction.

Where do we begin? First, we Sherlock Holmes the names, as you learned to do in Chapter 2. Mac: tough, working class, older generation name, masculine, cop, fireman, old school, integrity. His last name is Taylor. Does he "stitch" clues together? Instinctively, we know who he is and what it is about (and more if we've previously watched the show). What about the name Stella? Sounds Italian or ethnic in some way. It's classical. If you know Italian or Google it, you find out it means "star." She's probably beautiful. Feminine. Her last name is Bonasera, which is a derivation of the Italian phrase *buona sera,* which means "goodnight."

Sharon is not one of the lead characters, but a guest on the program for this one episode. If you get the script and your character's name isn't one of the leads, you automatically know that you are there to serve them. On a crime show, like this one, if you're not police or legal/judicial, you're probably a suspect or a witness. Sometimes the meaning of a name comes from the sound. Shakespeare used to do that, and so do modern writers. Names are code. In this case, Sharon sounds like "share-on." Intuitively, we might guess that *she shares*. You might ask the question: Is she generous in some way?

There is a system in the brain that filters information from your environment out and in. It lets information that you believe is important pass through your mental filters, and actively seeks solutions that fulfill your needs. So always remember that by asking questions you are telling your brain to hunt for the answer because it's important to you. If you don't ask questions, you won't notice the answers you need in the script.

And by the way, you should say your questions aloud. That slows you down to the speed of conscious thought (as opposed to the light-speed pace of subconscious thought) where you can participate in the investigation of your script on more than an instinctual level. Speaking aloud to yourself also tells your brain, "This matters to me."

Having done an intuitive assessment of the name of the show and the names of the characters, followed by having ascertained where you are (in the kitchen that also serves as Sharon's workplace), you can then move on to our next question.

What Page Is This Scene on?

The page number locating the scene you are to read in the script matters. This tells you where you are in the plot: Is it Act 1, Act 2, Act 3, the opener, or the teaser? So ask: "What page is it on?"

In the case of our *CSI: NY* scene, the script tells us we are on page 10. Discovering this fact should prompt you to ask a next question: "What happened between page 1 and page 9?"

* In most TV scripts, there is generally one scene per page. Although this particular scene runs two pages long, it's feasible that this is scene 10. Not all of those other scenes necessarily have to do with this one plot, as one-hour TV dramas often have intertwined plots: an A plot and a B plot. But you can deduce from the page number that information was given about a murder, which is now being investigated.

You, the actor, don't yet know what the crime is, or how your character is related to Mac and Stella's investigation, so you want to stay on the alert for plot-related facts.

What Has Already Happened?

As an actor, you should go from line to line looking for clues of what has happened prior to this scene—both in the scenes the viewers will have seen and in the earlier life of the character. You want to know what every word means to your character. But you also want to allow your character to evolve with the lines. The first time you go through the script Sherlock Holmesing it, you won't know more than your character knows in the scene you are in or on the line you are on. Your impressions during the first reading are enormously valuable. As an actor, you may have a hunch about what happened, but you must be on the lookout for confirmation as you continue reading. Later when you go to rehearse the scene, knowing where your character was surprised or where you, the actor, had a hunch confirmed gives you an opportunity to craft a special moment. The writer intends for information to be made evident to the audience on a certain schedule.

Some actors believe that if they had the whole play or episode to read before their audition they would do a better reading. But this is not true. You cannot play the plot. You have to play each line as it comes. The adage "Ignorance is bliss" applies to acting.

As you know, when Sharon says her first line, it gives us a ton of information. She's been "at work" taking photographs in the kitchen. And when Mac replies with the second line of dialogue ("We won't take up much of your time") we know even more. The writer is telling us that Sharon already knows Mac and Stella.

Stella has the next line, which is a question about the Marathon. She wants to know if Sharon volunteered there. And she also gives away that it was "yesterday." When Sharon responds we learn that, yes, she was a volunteer, and she does the same every year. She also asks if it's okay to sit down because one of her legs is injured. The script indicates that a flashback will be inserted in the episode here showing how she got the injury: A marathoner racing in a wheelchair crashed into her. (Remember the ramps going from room to room that we flagged for inquiry when we first saw them described? Isn't it interesting?) Stella observes a bruise and persists in asking about it.

Sharon's next line includes a lie: She blames her injury on a runner, not a wheelchair. Stella, sensing an untruth, asks a question to confirm this explanation; and Sharon nods. So now you know that Sharon is lying; she's got a secret of some kind. But what?

Remember, one word in the script can make a difference. When an actor once asked him what something in his play meant, Harold Pinter said, "It's in the script." He meant, "Go find it. That's your job as an actor. I wrote it and now it's your turn." Acting is interpretation; it's making choices. And acting for the camera, as I intend to continue to reiterate, is about knowledge. On your first reading of these sides, you would already have seen different kinds of equipment and events depicted in the script, beginning with a camera with the "macro lens." If you don't know what that word means, you should go and Google it or Bing it on the Internet. It means, "Very close up."

Also, you learned about Sharon being at the Marathon (meaning the New York Marathon because the show is *CSI: NY*). What do you know about that event? She says there were 35,000 runners. She says she was volunteering at an aid station. You'll also observe in reading the description of the flashback scene, which takes place in the aid station where she was volunteering, that she was injured by a "cantilevered brake lever" on a wheelchair (something else to look up online). And she's told a lie. These are all clues that will become useful in your later crafting.

The next line Sharon has is a question aimed back to Stella. She changes the subject, by saying, "You said you had some questions about a cat?" Now we know how come she didn't ask Mac and Stella who they were in the first line: They had told her they would be stopping by to ask about a cat. But we don't yet know what that means, so we have to flag it as interesting. You would ask yourself: What happened to the cat?

As the dialogue continues, more facts are revealed:

The neighbor's cat died.

It scratched the screen on her window or door.

Her apartment is wheelchair accessible.

Photographic contact sheets (proofs) are of pictures of sushi dishes (raw fish).

While Stella continues speaking with Sharon, Mac looks around. He finds a "small compressed air canister." Sharon explains that it contains carbon monoxide to brighten the food she uses in her photographic shoots. *This must be significant information,* you should think, as an actor. *Let me flag that.* Then, go and investigate carbon monoxide online. You'll find out it is deadly. According to Wikipedia, it is a "colorless, odorless, and tasteless gas, which is slightly lighter than air. It is highly toxic to humans and animals in higher quantities, although it is also produced in normal animal metabolism in low quantities, and is thought to have some normal biological functions."[2]

These are your clues. What do they add up to? As an actor, you want to stack the deck in your favor by heightening the meaning of every moment. Therefore, you should be extremely curious about the reason homicide detectives are asking you about the cat. Cops don't normally investigate animal deaths. A human has died, and so has a cat. You have hidden the truth about how you were injured. Chances are you are guilty of killing the cat. But you don't know for sure, even by the end of this particular scene, based on the facts it provides you, how the cat's death is relevant to the murder investigation.

You wouldn't necessarily know ahead of your audition that killing the cat was a test run for poisoning someone with carbon monoxide spray. But you would know that Stella and Mac are looking for a murderer, and that Sharon could very well be a killer. A later scene reveals that Sharon lured her neighbor's cat to her apartment with tempting pieces of sushi, and then sprayed the cat in the face through the screen. Right now, in Sherlock Holmesing the script before taking the steps of crafting a performance, you are just gathering evidence. So far, you've learned a lot—although not everything. But the writer is not hiding anything from you. All you need to do this scene well is there, in the script.

Later on, you will craft the moments and make sense out of your clues.

Notes

- Start by SHing the names
- Use curiousity, intuition, deduction
- What page is this one
- What happened in the pages prior
- What script clues can help tell
  you what happened prior
- Use those clues to further learn
  what you did prior to this
  scene
- What is mentioned that you as
  an actor need to learn that
  your character knows
  ex. NY Marathon, Carbon
  Monoxide
  →

Notes

- What can you deduce
  from all the clues
- Who are you as a character
  and what is your role
  in this episode
- If not lead, you are there
  to serve the leads

CHAPTER 5
WHEN IS THIS TAKING PLACE?

> *Emotional release by itself, no matter how 'real,' 'honest,' etc. the emotion may be, is never enough to create a character . . . such release has no artistic form."*
> **—Richard Hornby**

If you woke up in the hospital with amnesia, some of the questions your doctor would ask you are: "Do you know what year it is? Do you know today's date?" Everyone whose faculties are intact has a sense of placement in time. Busy people might occasionally mistake a Tuesday for a Wednesday, or accidentally date a check September 15 instead of September 16. But it is unlikely that they would mistake the month, the year, the decade, the century, or the millennium. People know the season, too: knowing if it is spring, summer, autumn, or winter. If employed, they can distinguish between a weekend and a weekday (or in some cases, a work day and a day off). Unless they are underground or trapped in a room without windows, they usually know if it is night or day.

All these ways of keeping track of time are knowledge your character embodies, and evidence you need to collect before you can begin crafting your audition. For the purpose of a given role and to bring a script to life, you may benefit from determining:

- Time of day/night.
- Day of the week.
- Season.
- Year.
- Date of an event.

Time of Day

Contrast the experience of being in a graveyard at two in the afternoon and two in the morning. If you know from the script that your scene is at 2 A.M., this may hold an acting clue for you. Auditioning for a film or TV project, such as *Twilight, True Blood,* or *The Vampire Diaries,* you could make an educated guess that it is relevant to the plot that your scene takes place in the nighttime. Time paired with location can be a very revealing detail when dealing with subjects such as vampirism. For you see, vampires, werewolves, and spooks only come out at night. Might you be predator or prey, vampire or victim?

Or let's say that the sides you've been given are for a scene in a romantic comedy, like the 1993 film *Sleepless in Seattle,* which stars Tom Hanks and Meg Ryan. The final scene is a rendezvous at the top of the Empire State Building at closing time. Ryan's character, Annie, almost misses this appointment. Racing across town to get there before the man of her dreams leaves adds tremendous urgency to the action. In a plot twist, she arrives too late and is disappointed. They meet only because Hanks' character, Sam, returns to retrieve his daughter's lost teddy bear, which Annie has found on the floor of the observation deck. Off they walk, hand in hand. Time often adds urgency.

What about 3 P.M., the time of day when kids need to get picked up from school? How might this be relevant to your character's experience? If the character breakdown tells you that you're reading for the role of a stay-at-home mom, this could matter a great deal. It might also be significant to a schoolteacher or principal whose day with students is ending. What if the scene you're reading is between a teacher and a student meeting at 3:30? Might this scene be about mentorship, advice, discipline, an illicit affair?

If the writer gives you the time, you can be sure there is a meaningful reason.

Day of the Week

In acting, all knowledge is experiential. For a nine-to-five office worker, Monday morning—representing the beginning of the workweek—is a much different experience than Friday afternoon—the end of the workweek. If the screenwriter gives the day to you, it is probably going to factor into the plot. Make note of it. When you're crafting, you'll make a choice about its meaning and how to play it. If your character has a line like, "I hate Mondays" or "Thank God it's Friday!" you won't have far to go to find the feeling.

You not only need to know the day of the week or the time of day, as an actor you also need to understand what happens on that day or at that time. In the HBO television series *In Treatment,* starring Gabriel Byrne as a psychologist (Paul) struggling to confront issues in his own life in parallel to the lives of his patients, every episode is stamped at the beginning with a name, the day of the week, and the time of day. The final episode of each week in his life takes place on Friday at five. This is a session he has with his own therapist, Gina. For him, that day and time is highly significant. It's the session in which he exposes his feelings, rather than holding them back. If you were reading sides for a scene as Paul, you would need to know what this means to him.

What about Saturday night for a single person versus a married person with teenage kids living at home? Is the scene you are preparing for your audition related to looking for love, going on a date, or waiting for your kid to come home from a party? In the 1977 film *Saturday Night Fever*, written by Norman Wexler, John Travolta stars as Tony Manero, an uneducated store clerk from Bay Ridge, Brooklyn, for whom the highlight of his life is the one night a week he dances at the local discotheque. That one night, he goes from being nobody to being the king of the world. The difference between who Tony is being on Saturday and who is he being on every other day is central to every choice this character makes, and evokes his central struggle of wanting more out of life.

So ask yourself, what day does this scene take place? It is actable if you know what it means to your character.

Season

In spring, the Earth turns green again. The snow melts. The ground thaws. The sap rises. Tree leaves grow. Flowers begin to bloom. The birds and the bees procreate. And the human heart turns to love. School lets out. Graduations and marriage ceremonies take place. Baseball training camps open. Depending on who your character is, the season could have a variety of meanings. It might be intimately related to the plot, such as it was in 2007 film *Into the Wild,* written and directed by Sean Penn, based on a true story. Lead character, Christopher (played by Emile Hirsch), has crossed a river in Alaska to isolate himself in nature. When he runs out of food and attempts to cross back, he discovers that the water in the river has risen from the spring runoff. In the moment of his discovery of being trapped, he is devastated. Ultimately, he dies from eating a poisonous root.

Summertime is hot and sweaty. It's the season when most people take a vacation and kids go to sleep-away camp. The light of day lasts longer and people go outdoors—or they hide from the heat in front of an air conditioner. There are softball games and tennis matches to play, and backyard barbecues to attend. Baseball season is in full swing. Think of all the baseball movies you have ever seen: *The Rookie, The Natural, Eight Men Out, The Bad News Bears, Major League, Bull Durham, Field of Dreams,* and *A League of Their Own,* among others. At the beginning of the summer—near the start of the baseball season—you might have one kind of scene in such a film, whereas toward the end of summer—when the season is winding down and playoffs are coming up—you might have another. Activities your character engages in, and how your character experiences them, could have everything to do with the season of the year.

Season can dictate appearance. Autumn is a season of transition. The leaves are changing colors and there is great beauty in the environment, and the air is getting colder. The clothes that people wear are warmer. No more shorts and tank tops. On colder days, they wear coats and long sleeves, gloves and hats. Warmer days, which are known in North America as "Indian summer," elevate people's spirits and give them one last chance to frolic outdoors before the hibernation of winter sets in. In the 2010 independent film *Please Give,* Oliver Platt and Catherine Keener play a husband and wife who run a used furniture business in Manhattan. Going to see the autumn leaves serves as a metaphor for the capacity to enjoy life and hold an optimistic view. The couple is waiting for their mean-spirited next-door neighbor to die, so they can take over the grumpy old lady's apartment. In one scene, a row of people is standing on a hilltop looking at a magnificent view; the joke is that the old lady is looking the opposite way and misses the beauty. The fact that it was autumn helped to define an important aspect of the character of the elderly woman, and contrast it with the character of her sweet-natured granddaughter, who is trying very hard to please her and help her have a positive end-of-life experience.

Winter. Watch the 1997 movie *The Ice Storm,* directed by Ang Lee. Set during Thanksgiving week 1973, it depicts an entire subculture of white, middle-class, suburban Americans amidst the political malaise of the Watergate scandal and the changing social and sexual roles of that era by focusing on the activities of one dysfunctional family in New Canaan, Connecticut, on one evening. On this particular night, there is a dangerous storm, which affects each of them literally and also is a metaphor for the period. As in *Into the Wild*, the havoc wreaked by the storm causes several major plot twists: Paul, the son of the Hood family, gets stuck on a train coming home from Manhattan; a power line broken by a fallen tree limb electrocutes Mikey, the eldest son of the Carver family.

Also think of the road-trip buddy movies that begin with people who can't get a flight out of an airport. *Planes, Trains, and Automobiles* with John Candy and Steve Martin is one such film where the weather forces an unlikely pair to rely on each other. Because winter is the season of Christmas, Hanukah, and New Year's Eve, winter has cultural and religious significance that could factor into the scenes you might be called to audition for. When you see winter in your sides, your job will be to deduce its relevance to the actions of your character. Read the lines to confirm any intuitive guesses that you make.

Year

Historical dramas are perhaps the most obvious example of projects in which the year matters. Director Martin Scorsese has made many such films: *Raging Bull*, a biopic about Jake LaMotta, a champion boxer in the 1940s; *The Last Temptation of Christ*, set in the biblical era; *The Age of Innocence*, a costume drama set in the 1870s; and *Gangs of New York*, set in 1862. There are also television series, like *Rome*, which are set in places of historical relevance. When a project for which you are auditioning is set in a period earlier than our own—and for us, this means any year preceding the last ten years—you can be sure that the era has clues for who your character is *being.* Every period in history has its own social customs, values, and mores. As an actor, you need to figure out what these are. In Part Two, we'll look at crafting behavior that is appropriate to different historical eras.

Granted, today we look back at *Saturday Night Fever* as a film revealing the culture of the 1970's disco era. But don't forget that at the time it was made, it was current. If you had auditioned for it, you would not have had to adapt your behavior to the year, only for the subculture of the disco or Brooklyn. *The Ice Storm,* by contrast, looked backwards from its own year, which makes it a period film and a commentary to contemporary viewers on what we can learn from it. How did men and women interact then? What was it like growing up then? What were the concerns of the people in that place at that time? As an actor, you'll take the clues of the era that you find in the script and craft from them in ways that humanize them. Don't get too intellectual and heady about it; you just need to know how it informs body language, speech, and values.

Costume can help you find your period adjustment when you are performing, but I would not advise walking into an audition room wearing full period dress. I had a student who went to an audition for Arthur Miller's play *The Crucible,* which is set in Colonial America. Someone else who was there did the "cobra head," a 1990's gesture. That was a dead giveaway that the actress was not connected to the era of the play.

Generally, the social dictates for a leading character in a historical era are the main source of that character's conflict. For instance, a woman who wants freedom in an era where women are subservient to their male relatives has a desire that is in direct conflict with the customs of her time. *Roots* was a mini-series about the lives of a black family in America descended from an African man forced into slavery, which demonstrated their immense challenges in life up through different decades. If you were auditioning for a project like this, you would want to know everything about the decade of your scene.

Being gay and wanting to live openly and have full civil rights was the central theme of *Milk,* which was set in the 1970s. Some of the characters were gay activists in San Francisco. Others were not. They were politicians, news reporters, and anti-gay rights activists. If you are auditioning for a character that is not the lead, your character may be there, in the scene, to serve as opposition to the lead actor or to reveal something about the customs of the period. What does the year have to do with who you are to be?

Finally, some projects—especially science fiction projects—will be set in the future. Determining the common references and customs of this speculative period is something that a good screenwriter will provide. Look for those clues. If earlier episodes of a TV series are available to you, study them to see if you can determine an underlying set of principles of behavior to which you must adhere. Hopefully, the character breakdown will also give you insight into the values and customs of the people of this future. Don't make it up; use the script for guidance. When you get to the step of crafting from the sides of your audition, you will find ways to personalize the lines. We'll explore how to do so in Part Two. For now, keep looking for clues to what your character knows, as the camera sees knowledge.

Date of an Event

The scene from *CSI: NY* that we looked at in the previous two chapters is a good example of how the time of occurrence of an event can be meaningful to a character, and also be central to the plot. When an event is mentioned in a script it is a fact worth noting and worth understanding in detail. A future event is something your character knows and anticipates. A past event is something your character knows from memory. In this case, we know that the murder being investigated took place at an aid station at the New York Marathon. It occurred "yesterday" for Sharon, Stella, and Mac. Because this is a real annual event, your research should include knowing as much as possible about it.

As a contemporary actor you have invaluable resources available to you: YouTube, Google, Bing, Wikipedia, streaming news reports, libraries full of books, and websites of event-related organizations, like The New York Road Runners Club, which hosts the Marathon every year. You can go online and view pictures of the Marathon from years past. See if you can get some ideas about the weather and the people. What do people wear at this event? How do they behave? When does it start? When does it end? How does the "aid station" mentioned in your sides function? What is it like to volunteer at the Marathon? These are things your character absolutely knows, which would be parts of the answer to the question: When does this scene take place?

Everyone can remember important events from his or her life (birth of a child, graduation, marriage, divorce, being fired, getting hired, or the death of a loved one). So the answer to when is this script taking place, might be: "On the day before my wedding," "The morning after a drunken one-night stand," or "Three minutes after waking up from a coma." People also remember highly significant social and political events that took place in their lifetimes, as would your character—events like the 1929 stock market crash, the 1941 bombing of Pearl Harbor by the Japanese, the 1963 assassination of President John F. Kennedy, the first moon landing in 1969, the Challenger Disaster in 1986, and the 9/11 attacks in 2001. If a script references any kind of event, your job is to deduce what your character knows about it—as much as that which the character does *not* know about it.

When Was the Script Written?

Most sides have a date printed at the top of the first page. The date on the script is a small, but important clue. In the case of the *CSI: NY* script, the date printed on the sides is 6/30/06. This is not the same thing as the air date. It is the date the script was finished being written. And it means that nothing you act from the sides can have taken place after June 30, 2006. Make no reference in your work to things that happen later than that date.

Once you have identified all of the parts of "when" in the script, you will have choices to make about how to act the role. If the scene takes place in the past, you will have to find the way the people then behaved, carried themselves, or experienced life because of living in that time in the place or subculture of which they are a part.

Notes

CHAPTER 6
WHO AM I?

Acting is a question of absorbing other people's personalities and adding some of your own experience."
—Paul Newman

In the mid-2000s, I had the privilege of coaching Robert Wisdom on how to audition. At the time he already had a body of professional work under his belt, obvious talent, and he was ready to boost his career to the next level. By embracing the self-same tools being offered to you here, he went on a booking spree, delivering excellent audition after excellent audition. In his own words, "My confidence, my grounding, and my booking went up 300–400 percent after working with you. I literally went five months and booked every job, and I was turning down jobs." You may be familiar with Robert's television career of the past few years, which includes starring roles on series like *The Wire, Prison Break, Supernatural, Happy Town,* and *Burn Notice*; his resume of films includes roles in *Ray, Barbershop 2, The Collector,* and *Freedom Writers.* Now he has an enviable career.

When you look at any actor's career, it is fun to study how the actor transforms while he remains truthful to his own nature. Robert is a perfect case study. From playing Howard "Bunny" Colvin, a frustrated major in the Baltimore Police Department, in *The Wire* (HBO); to playing Norman St. John, an incarcerated Panamanian drug lord, known by the other inmates by his street name, Lechero, in *Prison Break* (Fox); the angel Uriel in *Supernatural* (The CW); and Vaughn, a disingenuous spy handler, in *Burn Notice* (USA Network), we often see the same gentle smile and authority that are aspects of Robert's own temperament channeled through the different characters he portrays. Most importantly, you always see something alive behind his eyes: his knowledge of who he is and the situation, and clarity about the moments in the scene. He understands how to use himself truthfully to satisfy his circumstances as they are given to him by the writers. His crafting is specific and then he leaves himself alone, trusting it will be there for him.

After the early cancellation of the show *Happy Town,* he told Neal Conan, host of National Public Radio's *Talk of the Nation,* "You know what? In this game, you just keep pitching. You know, you walk away, you dust off, and we're right back in the game."[1] The same philosophy is applicable to doing an audition: Do your work as well as you can today, walk away, do it again the next day, and keep on playing the game.

So how does an actor of Robert Wisdom's caliber answer the question "Who am I?" when he reads the sides? The same way you're going to do it: through investigation. Thus far, you have intuitively and deductively reasoned your way through five elements of the script. You therefore have determined the project, your name, where you are, what has already occurred, and when the scene is taking place. All of this information is cooking inside you, and you might be tempted to jump ahead and make decisions about how to play the scene. Here's where it pays to slow down and really commit to the process of deduction. Knowing who you are informs your relationships and your conduct.

The breakdown for Wisdom's role in *Prison Break* might have read like the following description taken from Wikipedia: "A Panamanian drug kingpin incarcerated at Sona, where he is the leader of the prison and is at the top of the prison hierarchy. Sona prison has been run by the inmates and guarded only from the outside since a riot the year before. Ruthless and violent, he earned the nickname 'Lechero' when he, at the age of thirteen, disguised himself as a milkman in order to kill his mother's rapist."[2] It might also include details, such as this one from the Internet Movie Database: "Lechero has a powerful network inside and outside the prison. He has the only means of communicating with the outside world, a cell phone."[3]

Among other things, from this information you would discover the need to speak your lines with a Panamanian accent. Obviously, you'd have some homework to do. First, you'd pull out an atlas or go online and find a map of Panama. You'd discover that it is the southernmost country in Central America, bordered by Guatemala to the north and Colombia to the south. Its climate is tropical maritime, very hot and humid. The official language is Spanish. You might also discover (or remember) that in 1989, the United States deposed a dictator in Panama named Manuel Noriega. Although it is a tiny nation, Panama is strategically important because it controls a canal, which is the only passage by water from the Pacific Ocean to the Caribbean Sea, the Gulf of Mexico, and the Atlantic Ocean. Nearby, in the north, lies a string of islands, the largest of which are Cuba, Jamaica, and Dominica (home to Haiti and the Dominican Republic). Robert Wisdom's parents both come from Jamaica, and the accent he ultimately used for the role sounds a bit Jamaican.

"Who am I, if I am a drug kingpin?" you might ask. "And who am I if I am the leader of a group of violent prisoners who run their own prison?" If you use your intuition, this is where it will help you find an approach to your character. If this is who you are, you are a powerful man. Commanding. Not to be messed with. Capable of meting out punishment. Someone who rose to the top by fighting your way to the top. You've seen violence and done violence. Dominant. Controlling. Intelligent. Your word is the law. A dictator. As John Kubicek of BuddyTV reports, in an interview about his approach in *Prison Break* Wisdom told him Lechero was "based on or inspired by a number of historically ruthless dictators, such as the Shah of Iran, Idi Amin, and Benito Mussolini. In other words, Lechero is not someone to be taken lightly."[4]

Knowing who you are is essential to understanding your relationships with the other characters in any scene you are playing. It gives you avenues for exploration when you go to do your crafting. It tells you what you to need to study.

Of preparing the part of Major Colvin for *The Wire,* a career cop who wants to make a difference before he retires, Wisdom says: "I have to say that the Baltimore police force was really great. I hung out a lot with them. We did a lot of ride-arounds. I spent a lot of time in West Baltimore, which is a pretty rugged area. And they taught me a lot. They shepherded us through. And, you know, I have the utmost respect for the work that law enforcement does across the country, and primarily due to the show."[5]

For *Burn Notice,* where in the fourth season he plays Vaughn, the handler of the lead character Michael, whom he lures into an unsanctioned clandestine operation by telling him they are hunting for a terrorist mastermind, he said: "I'm playing an old-school spy, Cold War spy, who is now a wolf in tiger clothing. And it's a great big, fun role."[6] And it is fun, as you read a script, to ask, "Who am I? Who do I get to be?"

Look for Your Answers Beneath the Lines

Cast your mind back to the role of Sharon, the photographer, in *CSI: NY.* There is a second scene she appears in that we haven't yet discussed; this one takes place in an interrogation room at the police station. During this exchange, Stella presses Sharon for an admission of guilt. She knows how Sharon did it, but not the reason why. The sides include inserted flashbacks of her murdering a runner named Owen Reid at the aid station in the New York Marathon where she was passing out water. As he reaches for a cup of water, she sprays his face with a cold blast from the canister of carbon monoxide.

Remember how the cat was poisoned?

In this scene, details are provided about the plot, from which you could deduce who she is: Her brother is a top wheelchair racer, and he used to be an All-American runner. Owen Reid was a drunk driver who crashed into his car and, as she says, "took my brother's life away." In this scene, she confesses her motivation to murder him came from revenge for what happened.

On the surface of the lines, you have a number of clues about Sharon. She is:

- A photographer.
- A devoted sister.
- A marathon volunteer.
- A murderer.

When you are looking for clues about who you are, however, remember that the dialogue only provides plot details. But you cannot act the plot. Dialogue is only what is said. Reality is created by emotion. Finding who you are is something that you will have to discover underneath the lines. It's relevant to your scene or scenes from the audition sides, because it's something in your character's history that leads you to make the behavioral choices you make in the events depicted in the script. This background is something you can create to stack the decks for yourself emotionally. But never forget, even if you make up parts of your history, the details must be supported by the script.

In the history of Sharon's life, the relevant details of her identity (some given in the script, some made up by you) could include being a woman who was building a career for herself when a terrible car crash occurred. A drunken driver slammed into the car her family was traveling in. Her parents died in the crash. Her brother was crippled. Now she is his caretaker and so, in effect, her own "life was taken away." Where Sharon (Share-on) is generous, the drunk driver Owen (Ow-in') may be a miser or a cheat. What if after the crash he agreed to pay a settlement, but he never actually paid the money?

Those ideas would not be in conflict with the sides. Some are provided. Others are embellishments that give you a strong point of view. Knowing these details will help you, as an actor, to know why you are bitter enough to seek revenge for something that happened to your brother. Because, you see, in this way it can have happened to you, too. You lost parents, life, freedom, and so forth, all because this schmuck, this villain, this guy who gets to keep running marathons, ir-responsibly—selfishly—caused a car crash and got away with it as if the event has not touched him. That's why you decided to execute him at the New York Marathon: He was *"owing."* You made him pay.

Who are you? The sword of justice. An avenger. A wronged sister. A justifiably and murderously angry victim.

The question of who you are is like an octopus with many tentacles. It could include:

- Gender.
- Sexual orientation.
- Age.
- Familial relationship.
- Location.
- Time.
- Events (past and future).
- Profession.
- Condition (drunk, stoned, injured, ill, mentally impaired).

When you see a clue in the script like that of having a wheelchair-accessible apartment, you have to wonder why. Nothing in the script—at least if it is relatively well-written—is ever arbitrary. You must always ask: *If this is true in my life, who am I?* Keep questions about details such as this open until the script answers them for you. Then you can do the next step of using them to define the reality of your situation for yourself. Use them to make sense of your emotional state and your character's choices. Once you have clarity, all of that knowledge will show up for the camera in the life behind your eyes.

Notes

Notes

WHAT DO I WANT THIS PERSON TO UNDERSTAND ABOUT ME?

> *In 'real life' the mother begging for her child's life, the criminal begging for a pardon, the atoning lover pleading for one last chance—these people give no attention whatever to their own state, and all attention to the state of that person from whom they require their object."*
> **—David Mamet**

Have you ever been pulled over by a cop on the highway? Reminisce for a moment or two how your behavior changed. Every move you made was careful: how you reached for your purse or wallet to get out your license, how you opened the glove compartment to locate the car registration. You spoke in a respectful tone of voice. Internally, you may have been anxious, but you didn't want that to show. Perhaps there was something in the car that you didn't want the police to see, like an open bottle of beer. Maybe you had several outstanding parking tickets or you knew you were speeding. Perhaps you hoped you would be let off with a warning instead of a ticket. Maybe you tried to be friendly, funny, or seem responsible, or you played dumb or expressed remorse in order to get a favor in return and be allowed to continue on your way with the least hassle and delay. This is an example of how behavior changes depending on the object of your attention, and what you want this person to understand about you to accomplish a specific result.

Now change the cop in your imaginary scenario to your elderly grandmother. How would you speak to her if she was the object of your attention? What about your six-year old son . . . or your fifteen-year old son? How about your lover—or a man or woman you are attracted to? What about your former wife or husband? How would you speak and behave to all of these individuals? Partly it depends on your subjective point of view about them; meaning, your feelings. But doesn't it also depend upon the circumstances in which you find yourself; meaning, what you need?

For the purpose of auditioning on camera, there are two pieces of information—*of knowledge*—that you need to draw forth from the script, which will help you quickly and clearly establish and bring to life your character's relationship with anyone in a scene. As you continue your Sherlock Holmesing, you must ask and answer:

- What does this person mean to me (my character)? Implicit in this question is the idea of your character's relationship to this person: my boss, my best friend, my arch rival, my stalker, my doctor, my potential investor, my interrogator.

- What do I want/need this person to understand about me? Implicit in this question is the idea of your character's objective in the scene: to impress, to comfort, to win, to evade, to get help, to be approved, to go free.

As an actor, knowing who you are speaking to is essential because it causes your behavior to shift accordingly. In Part Two, when we explore how to craft your audition, we'll go into the process of working imaginatively in order to find the exact significance of the people, places, things, and events you identify in the script, and bring this to life in the way you respond to them. That is a skill known as *personalization.* Who is this person to you? What does he or she mean to your character? Once you pick it, you can daydream about it. We'll talk more about personalization in Chapter 9, "Find Reasons to Feel."

Here, since you are still ferreting out the clues in your script, do your best to remain in the curious, intuitive, and analytical modes until you can answer this chapter's leading question: *What do I want this person to understand about me?* Not only do you want to determine if the script says you are speaking to your mother, for instance, but also that you want your mother to understand that you're not a child any longer . . . or that you respect her . . . or that you will take care of her now that she's old . . . and so forth.

In every scene you do for an audition, you need to know exactly who the object of your attention is, for your primary reason to do this scene is to cause this person—*the object of your attention*—to understand something specific about you. You must capture the other character in the web you are spinning for the purpose of achieving this goal of being understood—like a spider would a fly. That is where the scene takes place.

Some actors approach the capture of other actors in an almost adversarial manner. Before shooting a particular scene for a film, Sean Penn is reported to have remarked about a fellow actor, "I am going to eat him for lunch." I believe Penn knows about the web.

Russian actor/director Konstantin Stanislavski, whose method is the foundation of modern acting, had an expression he used to describe the importance of the interaction between actors; he called it the "magic circle." Within this circle, imaginary life—a full-blown reality—can be created. If you want magic to occur in your audition, you must create such a circle with your reader. This is a sacrosanct dimension in which it is best if you commit to working only to please yourself and fulfill your own sense of truth. When you do so, this makes the producers of the project feel secure about your work.

Your Reader Is Your Lifeline

The foundational reason to do a scene is because of who that other person is to you (think: *the reader's character*). It does not matter who, in reality, is sitting in that chair opposite you in the audition room; it could be a man or a woman, a flat-voiced reader or an animated reader. Just aim to capture the reader and do your audition for him or her. Even if this individual doesn't give you the ideal reading that you're hoping for, if you're committed to being understood in a specific way in the scene you're performing your intent will come across on screen. The camera records your every thought.

Though the theatrical instinct of actors trained in stage craft is to play to all of the people in the room, in an on-camera film or TV audition, in point of fact this propensity is counterproductive because the camera that is filming you is always recording you and, thus, the viewer is taking you in from the reader's perspective. So it is important to ignore any observers who are present, and put your focus and energy where it truly matters.

Never look away from your reader. Never look up or to the side except to look at a specific object or person that is referred to in the script: a clock, the moon or stars, God, your fairy godmother, the CIA agent who is tailing you—or for remembering. (Of course, you don't always have to look away for memory; it's just a choice.) It is best only to do this once in a scene—at maximum. Otherwise, keep your eyes locked on the reader. Glancing away is a behavior that will make your character come across as nervous, shifty, or disengaged. Personality is communicated behaviorally. The reader is your life-line because you can always return to your knowledge about this person, and the camera will perceive it.

Susan Sarandon reportedly said, "Our job is to unzip ourselves for the camera." Close-ups allow us to crawl into your interior, and an audition is always a close-up on you. If you look away, you block our access to your emotions— or, in other words, fail to "unzip."

Most actors lose their auditions in only the first ten or twelve seconds after the camera starts rolling because that's how long it takes to create a first impression—if that long. But if you are clear about who you are speaking to right away, in the first moment at the very beginning of your scene, the people listening to you and watching you will know it. And if the old adage is true that "cream rises to the top," then you want to be specific enough in your acting choices to eventually become the "cream" of the film and TV industry.

Name the Object of Your Character's Attention

No matter what gender your reader is, or what position this person holds in real life (director, producer, leading actor), your reader has to become what you need him or her to become for the sake of your audition. You will respond and act toward your reader according to who you make the reader in your imagination. Ultimately the reality of the reader to you will be based upon the suggestion of the text. The fact of who this person is will not be an emotional decision; it is provided by the screenwriter. Just know it.

This is my father.

This is my boss.

This is my girlfriend.

This is my surgeon.

This is my business partner.

You should be looking for clues that define the nature of the relationship as well. It is your father who brutalized you as a child. It is your boss who drinks and passes out on the jobsite. It is your girlfriend who is pregnant and wants to get married. It is the surgeon who saved your life. It is your business partner who has been embezzling from you. Later on, facts like these will make it easier to craft imaginatively and to generate emotion.

Then, take a next step. Give the object of your reading a name that stirs up some life in you. Write down this name at the top of your script to remind you to let it be the very thing you think whenever you look at the reader. Be like a child on the playground calling another kid a name ("Hey, don't call me *that!*"). The name you pick should be a human universal, a thought everyone can immediately recognize on your face if you think it, such as, "Asshole!" Or, if the object of your reading is supposed to be a handsome man, in the margin of your script you might write: "Mr. McSteamy." And it could even be a sound, like: "Mmm. Mmm. Mmm," "Awww," "Grrr," or "Yuck."

Remember, whatever you choose, the meaning of that name for your reader is there for you to call up at the beginning of your scene, and again throughout the remainder of your scene. Knowing this name can be especially helpful during moments of listening.

A little trick you can employ when you're auditioning is to silently add this name to the end of every line: "Hi there *(asshole)*." "What did you have for breakfast *(asshole)?*" Try that out in a rehearsal to see if you like the quality it adds to your delivery.

You'll know you found the right name when it changes your physicality. This isn't something you can fake—or would ever need to. Muscles hold memory. If you're relaxed and allow yourself to be affected by the input of your thoughts, your body responds. This is so simple a technique that describing it is, in fact, more complicated than doing it.

Having found your answer for the first question, "What does this person mean to me (my character)?" it's time to begin sleuthing clues in the script that address the matter of the second question, "What do I want/need this person to understand about me?"

Find Your Character's Through-line

Your through-line in any scene you play is going to be that which you want to be understood about you. Usually the clue to what this is can be found on the last page of the sides or toward the end of the scene. Almost all scenes in movies and TV shows start where they end conceptually. They are economical and have small developmental arcs. They are also archetypal: There are white hats (good guys) and black hats (bad guys). Relationships are simple: Dialogues take place between husband and wife, mother and son, lawyer and client, brother and sister, lover and beloved. What you want will be something evident. And by the end of the scene either you'll get it or you won't.

A cop interrogating a criminal, for example, might want the criminal to understand: "I will never stop pursuing your case until I have enough evidence to put you behind bars forever." The criminal in reverse might want the cop to understand: "You can't hold me."

Can you see how those two characters are having a contest where both cannot win? That's one important source of the dramatic tension in their relationship.

If your character ever says, "I need..." then you may have already found the very thing that your character wants to be understood. Sometimes it is communicated by the lines. But often it is left unsaid. This desire underlies all of your behavior in the scene.

According to the American Film Institute, for screenwriters, the "dramatic through-line of a script encompasses the premise and all the obstacles the protagonist will face."[1] Their job is to hinder characters (protagonists and antagonists alike) from getting what they want so that the audience of filmgoers or TV viewers can have the pleasure of watching them struggle to overcome their obstacles. But you, as an actor, are not fulfilling the same function as a screenwriter. For actors, the through-line of the scene is linked to the *super-objective* of what the character needs to *accomplish in life.* You aren't working to serve the needs of the script, but of your character's reality.

What's the difference between an objective and a through-line? In one scene from a typical script, a criminal is detained at the police station and then released because a judge has ruled some evidence—perhaps a gun—inadmissible in court. For the moment the cop's objective to arrest the criminal is frustrated. Nonetheless the through-line of being understood as "never stopping the chase" can be successfully accomplished.

Having a desire to be understood is not the same as having *an objective.* An objective leads a character to take action—to do things in the moment—whereas a through-line leads to thoughts: signs of knowledge behind the eyes that can be picked up by the camera. An objective is to make an arrest, by questioning, fingerprinting suspects, interviewing witnesses, and so forth. A through-line runs on a parallel track.

The through-line is always going to be a universal human need that is present within a character. And for the purpose of an audition, let's agree that this need will always be about the people in the scene and their relationship to each other rather than about the plot. Through-line explains *why* your character does and says things. It also explains what motivates your character to pursue certain objectives, which is why it is related to the super-objective—or the overriding goal that must be met by the end of the script.

In a well-written script the super-objective will be the reason that your character gets embroiled in any dramatic conflict. The need for this objective is a source of tension in every scene due to your character's circumstances: meaning, who you are, where you are, what has already happened, and who you are speaking to—all of that great information you've been pulling out of the script.

How do you find your character's super-objective? Simple. Work backwards from the conflict. If you can't find a conflict, then the script sucks. Invent one. Pick something.

An actable need could be: "I need you to see that I am better than you."

Once you discover what you want to be understood, you can run the scene and add a line stating the need to the tail end of your other lines as an exercise, like I suggested you do with the name you selected for the reader. Go through the script line by line, and after every line add the need as a mantra. Say it aloud. Notice how it colors your lines.

"Hi, I am Bob *(and I am better than you)*."

"Let's go to court *(because I am better than you)*."

You can practice this exercise at home as a rehearsal and go even deeper with the choice in your crafting. While Sherlock Holmesing the script, however, your main goal is to identify whether your chosen need rings true as an objective for your character.

On companion DVD 1 to this book, you can watch actors demonstrate the preceding exercise of specifying what their characters want the other person to understand about them. Pay at-

tention to the nuances of their physical behavior and vocal tones as they say the through-line aloud after each line of dialogue, and observe how those behaviors and tones remain in the subsequent reading that they do when it is implied, but not said aloud. Go to: TimPhillipsStudio.com/dvd.

Remember, it is essential to hit the notes that the screen-writer wrote. That matters! Your delivery in the audition—the emotional color you ultimately give to the lines—may not be the delivery that the writer originally intended, however, like a musician playing a piece of music you cannot leave out any notes that were scored for you by the composer. You cannot ignore the composition of the script and hope to give a successful audition.

Ideally, your need to be understood in a particular way by the person opposite you in a scene will be powerful because it is urgent as well as specific. Before your audition you have to know exactly what your character thinks is going to happen if you don't get what you want, as this knowledge heightens the dramatic tension of a scene considerably.

In the next chapter, we'll explore urgency and the matter of what's at stake.

 Notes

----

CHAPTER 8
WHAT'S AT STAKE IF I DON'T GET WHAT I WANT?

> *An actor is looking for conflict. Conflict is what creates drama."*
> **—Bette Davis**

Toward the end of the 2010 film *The King's Speech,* Colin Firth, who plays King George VI of England, is scheduled to give a radio speech to raise the morale of the British people. It's the beginning of World War Two and the situation is dire; the Germans are bombing London from the air. George's elder brother, David, has just abdicated the throne he only very recently inherited in order that he can marry a non-royal woman, and now George must make this speech. And he absolutely cannot fail because, if he fails, then the people won't accept him as their king. This is his chance to instill confidence, calm, and resolve in them to join together as a nation and stand up against the Nazis. It is also his opportunity to prove to himself that he is not "damaged goods" and is capable of leading.

The trouble is that George has a serious stutter. It is difficult for him to speak clearly, without stammering, and not to feel humiliated. He never trained to be king; nor did he develop an image of himself as being worthy of becoming king. His father berated him for having a defect and viewed his stutter as weakness of character. A private individual, giving a public address is perhaps the thing George fears most in his life, yet it is now the very thing he must do to fulfill his duty to his country and family. History demands it of him. Furthermore, as the first king in the modern era, he is being confronted with a new technology that broadens the scale of his possible embarrassment. He can't merely look noble sitting on a horse. He's got to use the broadcasting equipment and be heard by millions of his subjects simultaneously. Failure is not an option.

The personal and professional stakes are enormous. The pressure would be great under these circumstances even without a speech impediment to contend with, but due to the nature of George's physiological challenge—and the intimate story told around his efforts to compensate for it—the dramatic tension in the film is heightened. It hits an inspirational note when it comes to the scene where he gives the speech and triumphs. And because we know the dark events of the years that are right ahead of him, we love him for doing his duty. We are proud of him for doing his best. We love his humanity. And he comes truly to seem to embody a king by rising to the occasion that his life demands of him. But we also relate to his situation. We can see he's like everyone else. We would be like him if we had lived the same life as him, so his story is universal.

The script of this film is so successful at building urgency into the interactions between the characters it portrays that at the Academy Awards, Firth won the award for Best Performance by an Actor in a Leading Role. *The King's Speech* won Best Motion Picture of the Year. Tom Hooper won Best Achievement in Direction. And David Seidler, who originally saw the possibilities inherent in the meshing of the public and private sides of George VI's life, won Best Writing of a Screenplay Written Directly for the Screen. If you haven't seen it yet, watch it now to study how urgency factors into every scene. Read a copy of the shooting script (Newmarket Press, 2011).

It should soon become evident that in well-structured screenplays the clues you're learning to detect, intuit, or deduce are put together deliberately to raise the stakes for every character. Practice looking for this element in every film or TV show you watch.

If Colin Firth had played King George as if it was no big deal to give a speech, there would be no urgency for him to overcome his stutter. Urgency means your character is facing time pressure. Your objective must be reached by a certain time or date.

If war hadn't been declared or his brother hadn't abdicated his throne (or if that weren't a challenge to his sense of self), public speaking would have low stakes associated with it; the character would suffer no consequences, and the film would be dull indeed. High-stakes behavior comes from knowing and fighting to avoid certain consequences.

Having just determined your character's through-line in your sides—something you want and need the other person to understand about you—it's time to ask: *Why is this so im-*

portant to me? What's at stake if I don't get what I want? What will my life be like if I don't get it? The answer is your chance to increase the emotional energy in the scene.

Why Are You at a Crossroads?

As a rule of thumb, it's best to be simple when preparing scenes for an audition. What you know has got to be known down to your bones, so you should generally settle on straightforward answers that are easy to remember. Work with recognizable themes. Choose stakes that are human universals, which you can understand from your own life. For example, "If I don't get this, I'll never love again . . ." or "I'll lose everything."

On a fundamental level, a scene is always about either love or power. Which is it for your scene? Be curious. Aloud, ask yourself: "Is this about love or power? What universal human dilemma is this scene about for me?" An example of an appropriate response to these questions might be: "The scene is about love—love lost—and it's about betrayal. After giving my husband the best years of my life, he has betrayed me." The clues you need lie both in the character breakdown and in the text of the scene itself.

As we all painfully learn in our lives at some moment in time, people are what they do, not what they say. So you may find your clues to the stakes and the urgency behind the words, in the descriptions of the character's behavior or of the setting of the scene. For instance, there could be a digital clock ticking down the seconds on a loaded bomb. Your character has to defuse it before it detonates. Or your character might repeatedly be looking at his wristwatch. Your job will be to take those clues you find in the script and add them up to portray recognizable behavior. How does your character show urgency?

Urgency and high-stakes behavior can be serious or humorous. It all depends on the context in which it occurs. Jason Alexander, the actor who played George on *Seinfeld,* plays urgency and high stakes in non-urgent and ordinary moments, as if they are for real. In one scene George is yelling out of the window of Jerry's apartment at someone down on the street who is taking a parking space he wants. It is hysterical because he cares so deeply about something people normally treat as a mundane experience. Alexander worked against the grain like that on almost every line on *Seinfeld.* No matter what was said, he reacted to the private interpretation he gave to the other actors' lines.

There are two main ways to act comedy. The first is to act out a tragedy, such as by slipping and falling on a banana peel. People love to laugh at someone else's bad fortune. The second way relies upon your rigidity of purpose: You behave as if one simple goal must be accomplished or else you'll *die a hideous, untimely death.* Imagine what the picture of death looks like for you—those are your stakes. Alexander is really good at extreme ridiculousness.

In the theatre, applause is the reward you receive for acting. Applause comes as the curtain drops at the end of Act I or at the conclusion of the play. In film, the "applause" you get is an internal reward you give yourself when you hit the specific moments you planned in your scene. If you set up these moments well, you'll find that you can barely wait to do them in the audition. Nailing those planned moments is a sweet reward.

The producers and director who audition you are waiting for you to discover the important moments in the sides they've given you. If you miss the special lines that show you understand your scenes, you simply won't be hired. Discover your crossroads in each scene and it is going to be evident which lines are the main ones you need to "get."

You've heard me say that a scene is a compression of time, space, and reality. Urgency is one reason why. Here's another definition: A scene is the culmination of years of living that have brought you to the point where you are trying to get what you want *for a reason.* That reason is why you are at a crossroads in this one scene. And your character must do as Yogi Berra advised, "When you come to a fork in the road, take it."[1]

Let's break this definition down based on acting clues.

- You know who you are
- You know where you are
- You know what has happened
- You know when the scene is taking place
- You know what you want the other person to understand about you
- Now you are asking: *Why do I want this?* In other words, what's at stake?

Use your common sense to find your answer, which will be something on the order of: *Because I'll die. Because I'll lose my job. Because I'll never get another chance.* Notice how final these answers are. They're not wishy-washy. That's because this is a crossroads, not a traffic circle. You're supposed to go one way or the other, not to spin around and around. You're

108

fighting for survival, love, liberty, dominance, recognition, respect, relief, and all the things that motivate humans to take action when they do.

Stick to the basics. Every scene contains a dilemma that any human being could face. What this is must be crystal clear to you from moment to moment. But your job is not to act out the plot. Plot is a dangerous thing to focus on because a plot is composed of many moments, and you can only play one moment at a time. In every scene, the screenwriter backs your character into a corner from which you must escape. One scene, one corner.

Sometimes it's necessary to fill in the blanks of a poorly written script. When a script sucks, it's very hard to identify a crossroads for your character because the author simply didn't know how to create urgency or set up the stakes to add dramatic tension. Though I can assure you that in good writing these elements will be written into the scene, if you're auditioning for a part from an inadequately structured role—or going after a role with few lines—you have to add urgency and stakes for yourself using your imagination.

Invent an Actor's Secret

One way to add stakes to a scene is to invent an actor's secret. An older woman came to one of my classes with sides in hand for a role in a broad strokes comedy by the same producers who did the movie *The Hangover* (2009). Her character's name was Madge, and the role had a plain-spoken Thelma Ritter-esque comic quality to it. If you're too young to remember her, Ritter, a character actress of the last century, had a gravelly voice and a Brooklyn accent, and was well-known for stealing scenes in classic films like *All about Eve, Rear Window,* and *Pillow Talk.* Between 1951 and 1968, she was nominated for six Academy Awards for Best Supporting Actress, and numerous Emmy Awards.

When my student said her character's name was Madge, I immediately thought of the play *The Time of Your Life* by William Saroyan. Do you know it? That piece is a reflection of the 1930s, the years of the Great Depression. It's all about dreams never fulfilled, but never forgotten. There's a scene in a bar in San Francisco, where the leading character is people-watching. Based on the initials on the suitcase of a woman sitting nearby he comes up with the name Madge Lebowitz. He keeps guessing. I liken this image of a woman sitting alone at a bar to the Edward Hopper paintings of one person alone in a frame of a window in a diner or gas station. While Madge in *The Time of Your Life* is a woman in her thirties, I wondered if my student's character with the same name also had unfulfilled dreams.

The point is this. Auditions for roles like the one my student brought into class can be a chance for great character studies. Here are the clues we Sherlock Holmesed from the sides and character breakdown. Madge is a grumpy, gray-haired bank teller wearing a "perma scowl." She has three scenes set in a bank. In the first two, she's gossiping and snorting at things she's observing. The third scene takes place at night. In it, she is leveraging or blackmailing her employer, the bank manager. She says a line on the order of, "You owe me," which gave us the basis of a through-line for what she wanted him to understand about her: She wasn't taking no for an answer. It was time for him to pay her back. My student settled on: "I'm going to take you down."

For this particular audition, we decided she would establish an actor's secret to explain what happened in the past. She asked herself "Why does he owe me?" and worked backwards from there. Perhaps she saw the bank manager do something cowardly while the bank was being robbed and she never told anyone about it. And that was after years of tolerating him and waiting for her dreams to be fulfilled, like the people in the Saroyan play. Her dreams were never forgotten. The idea was for the secret to fill in the unknown elements in the lines. It could not conflict with what was there, but it had to have the potential to bring Madge to life.

We ran the scene in front of a camera. The first picture of my student's face showed us everything about her "payback" scene. She wore a look that read clearly on film: "It's my turn." She looked like Clint Eastwood in *Dirty Harry*. You know, the classic 1971 police thriller where he's a tough-guy cop in San Francisco who has no qualms about "blowing away" the bad guys with his revolver, after saying, "Make my day."

At the bottom of the scene, after all the dialogue was done she gave a little eyebrow twitch that communicated, "Take that, motherfucker!" I knew that if she trusted the work she'd put into the scene in class she would do an excellent audition.

On a side note, if you ever worry about being a character actor like this woman who was up for the role of a bank teller, just remember that "Twinkies" (super-pretty, young leading actors who look like fashion models) have to be surrounded by reality. Your character can provide it. If you count the number of actors on TV or in films who look like me and you (older, fatter, and balder, or whatever) you'll see we're in high demand.

My student James DuMont was cast in the role of a stock car racetrack owner in the film *Fast Girl* (2008). He phoned me from the set to help him find a way to approach a scene between his character and the character of young female driver, as he felt the scene wasn't working as well as it should. In the scene, the driver storms into his office and demands to be allowed to race, and his character tells her that because her father died on the second turn in his track a few years earlier he can't let her do it. James's issue was that he didn't have a sufficiently powerful reason to say those words. I suggested using an actor's secret to intensify his feelings. "She's your daughter." He skyrocketed after that.

Having discovered (or invented) urgency and what's at stake for your character in the scene, your Sherlock Holmesing is done and it's time to move on to crafting. While Sherlock Holmesing may be a relatively slow process as you learn it, with practice you'll be able to do it in less than ten minutes. It will become automatic, as will the process of crafting and making decisions about what to do with the knowledge you now possess.

Notes

 Notes

----

PART TWO

CRAFTING YOUR BUTT OFF

"No amount of skillful invention can replace the essential element of imagination."
Edward Hopper

"God took seven days to make the world. As an actor, you have to create a human being. That's no small potatoes either."
Tim Phillips

On the day of September 11, 2001, I was in my acting studio in Greenwich Village, a neighborhood not far from Ground Zero in Manhattan. The public transportation system had shut down. Thousands of people were migrating by foot northwards on the streets in varying degrees of shock. Many were covered in ashes. Seeing their plight, I hung a sign on the front door of the building that read: "Refuge here." This gave passersby the chance to come in, sit down, have some food and water, and clean up a bit on their way home.

Like many other people on that tragic day, I did whatever I could to help out—there was an outpouring of generosity that makes me proud. Even so, when I think of the firefighters who kept running back into the Twin Towers again and again attempting to rescue the people who were trapped inside those buildings before they collapsed, I am in genuine awe of their heroism. What they did on that day was important, and it was courageous. Their bravery and selfless professionalism in the face of overwhelming danger was a gift they gave the rest of us, and we should always remember to honor their contribution.

As actors, we are artists, meaning that we make a different sort of contribution. Although we are not in danger like firefighters, we also do important and courageous work;

something that's much needed in our society. Like emotional firefighters, we run into the "burning building" of our emotions so that others may feel. Most others run away, yet we choose not to. Our job is to run into the "fire" in order to reveal some form of knowledge, or meaning, and to do so in as entertaining a fashion as possible. In my opinion, this willingness to feel is a noble cultural service, because we do it on behalf of the audience.

The only reason to go into the "burning building" (which, in the case covered in this book, is your audition) is to truthfully represent the character that you are being asked to portray. If you take pride in your work as an actor, you'll never shirk this responsibility.

Think about it in the following way: If a film was being made of your own life, wouldn't you want your story to be told truthfully? Of course, you would. That's why you owe every character you portray the respect of delivering truthful life. This is your craft.

From the producers' point of view, you're like someone tossing them a life preserver: The water is rising and it's up to their necks. They are eager, even anxious, for their pilot to get picked up by a network, or they're worrying about money and time. In film and TV, time *is* money. They need to get a good performance from you, one that is truthful, specific. And they need to see that you have the capability to find the stuff that they put in the script for you, the clues for how to craft your performance. This doesn't mean you have to do the audition scene exactly as they imagined it; you might do it differently than they thought you would, but you have to show you found the clues in the way you craft your performance. If you do not, then the producers think you're not smart enough or good enough to do the part you're auditioning for.

Remember, you do not ever need to justify your work in an audition as long as it is truthful; simply come alive before the eyes of whoever is watching you. Your craft is not to "act," but to represent a human being in human circumstances. No matter what anyone tells you, as Robert Duvall says, "Protect your craft. It's the only thing you have in life other than time."[1]

Directors don't always know what to do. So if you blindly follow the director's lead without having thought through your role for yourself and made active choices, you could put yourself in a bad position. After all, who has to bear criticism for the portrayal on screen when the director gives you bad advice? You do. You're the one standing in front of the all-seeing camera lens.

Thorough crafting is how you can become director proof. My goal is for you to have pride of ownership in the role you craft, so much so that when you step into an audition room you can confidently state, "This is what I want to do with this role—and I can justify my choices in the script." That makes you a solid actor. All the great actors are solid in what they do.

In the good old days, we used to have to go in person to pick up our scripts. We had to walk up a steep hill—both ways going uphill—through the rain, tornados, and blizzards. Now sides get emailed to you or you download them. They come on your tablet or smart phone or computer. This seriously frees up your time to practice your skills, craft, and rehearse. Use your time wisely. Don't focus on being "right" or "wrong" from the producers' point of view. Be right for yourself, and then you'll be right for the script. Wrong choices are boring choices.

Gina Hecht, who plays the principal in *Hung* (HBO) and is a student of mine, told me that she now takes over the audition room when she goes in. "I am going to act in every audition because I am so sick of that audition *crap.*" She cuts lines sometimes, but, of course, always tells them what she's going to do before she does it. (I wouldn't recommend this unless you are very clear about *why.*) She takes charge of her performance. And she gets hired much of the time.

In an audition, the creative team and producers might ultimately want to see a *different* truth than the one you delivered, and they may ask you to make an adjustment, but they won't dispute or deny having seen truth when they see it. They're not there to tell you how to achieve results, only to select from among the truthful results presented them by different actors.

Emotion Creates Reality

You do not need to do a lengthy process of emotional preparation in order to prepare to perform well in an on-camera audition. Your life has been your preparation. Having thoroughly Sherlock Holmsed the script using your curiosity, intuition, and deductive reasoning, you actually have sufficient knowledge now to make some quick decisions that enable you to generate emotion in your body for the camera to pick up. You can access the emotions you need with the handful of simple techniques that you'll learn here in Part Two, "Crafting Your Butt Off." As you practice these on a regular basis, you'll come to trust them—and your ability.

Fundamentally, the responsibility of a film actor is to humanize the dialogue of the script, the whole time remembering that people are not what they say; they're what they do. Knowledge is the key. The task is to notice, "The writer gave me a word," and wonder, "How can I use that word to bring me to a specific choice that reveals the truth of a human being?" Then, when a choice has been made, the actor's job is to execute it clearly, transparently, so the truth can be seen on camera.

So how do you do that? Through crafting. To bring a role to life and create emotionally generated reality, you must master the art of bridging your body and psyche to your character.

Thus far, we've been talking about a special way to approach scripts that enables you to quickly draw out clues pointing you in the direction of credible choices. Now you'll learn to make bold choices just as quickly and bring your dialogue to life. You'll learn to rehearse.

When crafting an audition, the most important tools to draw upon are your imagination, your muscle memory, improvisation, and your ability to trust your choices and impulses. Being a student of human nature will come in handy, too; so will your degree of self-knowledge. You must be fiercely committed to following through on the screenwriter's intentions as you find them expressed in the script. If you are, the writers and producers you meet will appreciate your persistence. The number one complaint of casting directors is that actors are ill prepared.

Interestingly, a number of writers have sat in on my on-camera classes. When they came up to shake my hand at the end, they usually made comments like, "Thank you for showing actors how to act from my scripts." Some have said that understanding this way for actors to work from scripts has made them better writers. The eyes of one such writer were teary, as she gratefully told me, "Now I know what I need to go back and do in order to revise my new screenplay."

The point is this: You have the power to bring scripts to life. That's a gift.

Enter the Playground of Your Imagination

When it comes to crafting, the imaginaion is your playground. Just as astronauts use in-flight simulators to train for the things that could happen on their missions in space, you can use your imagination as your pre-audition experience simulator to generate the knowledge underlying the dialogue from testing different choices before you ever set foot in an audition. *Caution:* Never get stuck on having the scene go one way in an audition. An audition should be a journey of discovery.

Daydreaming is the activity you were sent to the principal's office for doing in class as a kid. I give you permission to start doing it again now. Give yourself daydreaming time with the sides. The business can erode your joy. You need to separate daydreaming time from doing business. You should commit at least half of your time to practicing your craft by hanging out in the playground of your imagination. You are an artist, therefore you need to daydream.

If we look just at the membership rolls of the two on-camera actors unions—the Screen Actors Guild (SAG) and the Association of Film, Television, and Radio Actors (AF-TRA)—we can estimate that for every actor who is working in a paid capacity there may be a hundred more who work only in nonpaying productions. If you got into this business to make big bucks, like George Clooney, Reese Witherspoon, or some other leading man or woman, how long did that motivate you? You've got to get back to the original reason you went into this business: to have fun. Acting is supposed to be fun. I know that the business can eat away at fun. That's why it's called "business."

The late Jerry Orbach, a well-known New York actor who played Detective Lennie Briscoe in the television series *Law & Order* for twelve years, was once filming on location in a Manhattan apartment building. A tenant engaged Orbach in conversation when he saw him waiting in the lobby for over a half an hour to shoot his next scene. The tenant asked, "Is it as tough as it looks to sit around on the set doing nothing like this?" Orbach responded, "That's why the producers pay me…" adding, "I act for free!"[2]

Many actors would share this sentiment. They love to act, and the love that they feel when they act shows in their work. Among other qualities, that's why we enjoy watching these actors on film; there is a kind of light and vitality in their eyes that is very attractive and compelling. Actors who have lost that delicious sense of joyousness and play have a real problem on their hands. Not only will their work suffer, but if they don't derive pleasure from every opportunity they're given to perform for the camera, no amount of money will ever feel like enough to compensate for the pain of waiting around for their chance to act—or for the need to audition.

Crafting is where the play enters into the audition process. Take the case of Meryl Streep. I only did one film with her, but I got to watch her crafting and playing. Though our scene ended up on the cutting room floor, it was a turning point for me to work with her for a full day on the film *Falling in Love* (1984). What I learned from the specificity she brought to her work impressed me. It was just the two of us. We were about four-feet apart seated across a desk from one another all day long, so I watched her. The story was that she was living in Connecticut, a graphic designer of some kind, and her marriage wasn't good. She was coming into New York City to be interviewed by me for a job in an ad agency. The reason the scene wasn't necessary was that it wasn't what the film was about, which was her romance with a man (Robert DeNiro) whom she met on the train.

Before the scene was shot, they brought Meryl prop drawings to use as her own. Her character was going to show my character her work. I watched her flip through the drawings in character and decide which ones her character would have drawn. I don't remember her saying anything about the reason for her choice, but before the camera rolled she'd decided on one drawing to show. It was magical to watch her process. She was definitive. She knew what she wanted.

Watching Meryl improvise around her choices proved to me that once you've done your homework on the script and you know who your character is you have a knowledge that is complete. That's when the self-expression and creativity of an actor enters into the process. Inspiration is not a godlike phenomenon, in my view. Crafting is. That's where technique occurs, the creative act. The play. An actor is on a quest to learn to speak with the voice of a character, to move with the body of a character—and to have that voice, that body be his or her own.

You need to act from a place of joy, self-discovery, and inner knowing for its own sake. So crafting has to be a part of your preparation. There's nothing worse than going into an audition underprepared. Not having found a particular way to play a scene and to behave as a character is excruciating both to actors and to the casting personnel who watch them audition. Crafting is where you put your insights about life in service to solving the problem of interpreting the script. You must be dedicated to this activity if you want to express yourself fully as an artist and as a professional. For as Marlon Brando once said, "To grasp the full significance of life is the actor's duty, to interpret it is his problem, and to express it his dedication."[3]

Trusting Your Results

The late Jason Robards, a renowned Eugene O'Neill actor, twice performed the role of Hickey in *The Iceman Cometh* on Broadway, thirty years apart, at its debut in 1956 and then again in 1988. When someone asked how come Hickey was different the second time around, he answered, "Life."[4] Robards wasn't trying to recreate his earlier performance as Hickey; he was not trying to find the "right" answers in the script. He was interpreting Hickey through the knowledge he'd developed of life and the world as he lived. I'm here to tell you that your knowledge of life is the ideal foundation for your acting, too.

Some actors, especially those who have not yet achieved success in the industry, feel a lack of confidence in their choices. Since they're not sure how to arrive at strong, specific choices, they frequently change course, retrace their steps, and gnaw endlessly on every decision. Self-doubt leads them to painfully criticize and second-guess everything they do. These actors are overly concerned about making mistakes and failing to gain someone else's approval.

The tools and techniques of crafting from your sides that you'll learn in the next several chapters can free you from unproductive work habits by shifting your focus to the things you actually can take charge of. They'll empower you to trust your choices and just get on with your acting. Perhaps most importantly, they'll help you to gain your own approval. They work.

After my student Renata Henricks won the lead in a pilot for a TV series she confirmed the efficacy of this way of crafting. She said, "The entire time I was auditioning I felt very relaxed about my work. There were much better known actresses than me in the waiting room and I was sure they'd get cast. After three rounds of auditions I still didn't think I could get the role. Then the casting director told me, 'Renata, it was amazing, but what you did just popped out on the camera. It leapt out at us.' I believe this came from not doing anything other than being truthful. When I learned how to craft, I began to trust my instincts more and do less. Now when an audition goes well, it feels as if I'm not doing anything special. I see that the point is to have everything crafted and then throw it away: just to breathe and to live and to do."

Trust can also be an issue for well-known actors. The super-successful Jayne Brook began working with me a few years ago after she had kids. We worked on character development in pieces when she'd already been cast in several episodes of *Private Practice*. She told me she wasn't having fun auditioning. Pre-children she didn't have to audition often because she'd take the lead parts in series. Now she just wanted to job in and job out and not carry a show, a decision that put her back into the cycle of casting. When Jayne took my audition on camera class, she complained, "It feels funny not to be working harder. You're making me do nothing. I'm afraid I won't do enough." I told her, "Believe me, you don't have to 'act.' Your choices will be there on camera." She was amazed at the natural quality of her work on the video playback.

What are the personality traits of successful actors like Jayne Brook, Renata Henricks, Meryl Streep, and Jason Robards? Obviously successful actors are more than "good looking." After all, there are lots of pretty people in the world. For certain they are driven and self-assured. Of course, they also have talent. They're born with the ability to access their imaginations and never have this ability drummed out of them as so many people in our culture do. Discipline is another of their personality traits: They respect the demands of the rehearsal process. In my experience they do whatever is necessary to find their moments and craft choices before the camera rolls.

Malcolm Gladwell asserts in his book *Outliers* that mastery of any skill or art form takes 10,000 hours. I tend to agree. Once you've had hours of practice, crafting will be as natural to you as breathing and you'll trust your results. Through discipline, you can become a master.

Notes

CHAPTER 9
CLICHÉS

Acting is a matter of giving away secrets."
—Ellen Barkin

One of the best, multipurpose shortcuts for on-camera acting I've ever seen is a tool called the *cliché*. From the French word for "stereotype," a cliché is a commonly used expression that everyone has heard or said so often that saying it aloud—or even thinking it—produces meaningful body language. Did you have the kind of mom growing up who could give you a specific look that meant you were in trouble? That's the kind of cliché you're looking for. I'm proud to say I invented this simple device, which is getting great results for my students in their auditions. Seriously, it's like a secret weapon.

In real life, when we're having a beer together and talking about our lives we talk in clichés. You describe a person you are dating. *Groan.* You slump over. You cover your eyes. Everyone understands exactly how your date went. The same is true in an audition. Familiar, frequently repeated phrases such as, "Easy come, easy go," "You'd better watch your back," and

"Put a sock in it," are actable because they're *human universals.*

Clichés can be used in several ways in a scene, including:

- To create full-blown life in the first moment.
- As the title of a scene, a through-line of objective.
- To develop your body language/characterization.
- As an expletive description for another character.
- Building an inner dialogue parallel to the script.

When rehearsing, you'll notice that some clichés mean more to you than others; not every cliché is useful for every actor. So when you find a cliché that works well, hold on to it: In future that's your golden ticket to generating clear, specific, animated moments. Clichés, like "Hold on to your horses" or "Whoa there," plainly bring actors to life.

Actors whose first language is not English frequently benefit from using clichés that come from their own cultures of origin. No matter where you're originally from, look for archetypal expressions so meaningful to you that they reveal themselves in your eyes and body.

Specific body language itself can be clichéd. There's the universally recognized symbol of "flipping the bird," which is the "Fuck you!" cliché of the raised middle finger. Of course, there are differences from culture to culture. My sister-in-law went to Africa and found out that an open-handed wave, which in America is friendly and means, "Hi there," in Africa means, "Your mother has five lovers." In sign language, this same gesture means, "All done," as in all done eating or all done taking a test. In Greece, it is symbolic of the curse word, "*Skata!*" and means, "Here's shit in your face."

Most actors will only ever need to identify a handful of clichés, because clichés can be recycled scene after scene, audition after audition, role after role. Before you settle on your favorites, I recommend that you set up a camera and film yourself reading the following list. These were compiled with help from actress Sherri Snyder. Have fun playing with them. When you look at the playback, observe how you were affected.

Just reading this list may cause you to remember others. As you go about your day, try to catch yourself using new ones. Keep a record here or in a notebook. Tracking these phrases is part of becoming a professional observer of life and human behavior.

Selected Clichés

Aha!

Back off!

Because I'm special.

Big fucking deal.

Well, what do you know?

What have we here?

Let me get this straight . . .

Come on, seriously.

Bullshit!

Busted!

Can't fool me!

Come to Mama, baby!

Could life get any better?

Cut me some slack here!

Damn it!

Damn, I'm good!

Day-um! (Damn!)

Don't even go there!

Don't get me started . . .

Don't you dare!

Don't you ever stop?

Duh!

Eat this, motherfucker!

Enough is enough.

Even better from behind.

Excuse me.

Excuse me for not jumping for joy.

Forget you.

Fuck 'em if they can't take a joke.

Get off my goddamned case already!

Get over yourself.

Give me a *[insert
   expletive]* break!
Go fuck yourself.
Go to hell.
Gonna get me some!
Got you there!
Got you where I want you.
Ha, ha. Fooled you!
Had enough or are you
   thirsty for more?
Hell yeah!
Hell-o!
Here comes trouble.
Here goes nothing.
Here it comes.
Here we go again!
How could you?
How do you like
   them apples?
How many times do I
   have to tell you?!
Hubba, hubba, hubba.
I always get my
   man/woman.
I could really get
   used to this . . .
I don't think so!
I got your number, bitch.
I know my stuff.
I know something
   you don't.
I'll get you yet!
I'll get you yet, asshole!
I'm better than you.
I'm gonna get it.

I'm in deep shit.
I'm the good guy here!
I'm the man!
I'm the shit!
Is that so?
It's all good.
It's always something.
Just you wait.
Lay it on me.
Let's get the fuck
   outta here.
Life's a bitch and
   then you die.
Mmm, mmm, mmm!
Music to my ears.
Nah-nah-NAH-nah-
   nah-NAH!
Nice ass.
No way!
Not on your *[insert
   expletive]* life!
Not so fast!
Nothing gets by me.
Now you've done it.
Nuh-uh!
Oh god, my baby!
Oh my god!
Oh no.
Oh shit!
Oh yeah?
Oh, come on.
Oh, fuck me!
Oh, yeah? What are you
   going to do about it?
Oops!

Poor baby.
Put a sock in it.
Right up my alley!
Score!
Silly me.
Sometimes I amaze
    even myself.
Sounds good to me!
Thank God.
That's what you think, pal.
There's a good little
    boy/girl.
This ain't my first rodeo.
This can't be!
This gets better and better!
Uh-oh!
Watch and learn.
Watch the master.
We'll just see about *that!*
We're screwed!
Well, isn't that special?
What do you say to that?
What else is new?
What gives?
What more could
    you want?
What the fuck?
What the hell do you

want from me?
What the hell?
What's happen-
    ing, hot stuff?
Where have you been
    all my life?
Whoo-hoo!
Yay me!
Yesss!
You and what army?
You got me there.
You just don't get
    it, do you?
You know how that goes.
You little shit!
You must be joking.
You the man.
You think I was born
    yesterday?
You won't [*insert exple-
    tive*] believe this!
You'd be surprised.
You're a dead man.
You're gonna pay.
You're so bad.
You're too much!
Yummy.

On companion DVD 2 to this book, you can watch actors demonstrating clichés. Go to: TimPhillipsStudio.com/dvd.

Now that we've identified a bunch of clichés, let's take a look at how to apply them in your work, starting right in the first moment of a scene.

Give Your Scene a Title

Every scene represents a universal human dilemma, which, at its basis, is either about love or power. This dilemma must be crystal clear to you (and, through you, to your audience) from moment to moment. If you don't show how you feel about what's going on, if you don't have this clarity, it's hard for anyone to take in your performance on film. As a rule, it's better to be wrong and be specific rather than right and general.

Clichés are specific. A twenty-something actress came to class with a scene from an actual audition she'd done for a bit part in the movie *Limitless,* which would be played against the lead actor, Bradley Cooper. His character, Eddie Morra (*more* intellect, *more* sex appeal, *more* everything, get it?) has taken a drug that makes him mesmerizing. In this scene, he picks up a woman up in a bar. He's accomplished, handsome, and smart—presumably everything a woman would want—and also successful in seducing her with minimal effort. So the title of scene we came up with for her was the cliché "I'd do him." As a rehearsal, I had her scan the reader from head to crotch once, and then stay fixed on his eyes. This, in combination with simply thinking the cliché, made her blush.

Please don't make the mistake of trying to play too many choices at once. Make one solid choice! Don't worry about being "too simple."

By its essence, a cliché is something universal that many different actors could play. But don't worry about coming across the same as someone else. No matter what cliché you choose (and despite its universality), that cliché is going to come across differently in your performance—in your body and voice—than it does in anyone else's. You can trust your own natural, very human and unique complexity to read on camera.

Song titles often make good scene titles. Just scanning *Rolling Stone Magazine's* list of the top 500 songs of all time, you could pick up a few possible choices, including: "She's Gone," "I Want to Hold Your Hand," "God Only Knows," "That'll Be the Day," "You Send Me," "I'm so Lonesome I Could Cry," "Born to Be Wild," "I Can't Stop Loving You," and more. Whenever you find a song title suitable for your title of scene, it means you've also found yourself a theme song or an anthem for an improvisatory rehearsal. Music is a great entry point to memory and emotion. They're hardwired into the history of our bodies.

Another place in popular culture where we find clichés is in standout lines from movies. What was the advertising for *Jaws 2?* "Just when you thought it was safe to go back in the water." That comes with the memory of the low, slow sound of danger: *dah-dum, dah-dum*, which we know means a shark is approaching.

Arnold Schwarzenegger gave us another cliché in *Terminator 2: Judgment Day* that's a possible title of scene when he said, "I'll be back." The more you look around for these types of clichés, the more of them you'll be able to collect. And each comes along with matching body language, and even a tone of voice, that is universally recognizable.

Here is a list of selected clichéd titles of scene (again, put together with assistance from Sherri Snyder) that you may choose from among. Or make up your own. Write them down here or in a notebook so you won't lose them.

Selected Scene Titles

Another Fine Mess You've
    Gotten Me into
Bring It on!
Ding Dong, the
    Witch Is Dead
Fasten Your Seat Belt,
    It's Going to Be
    a Bumpy Ride
Here We Go Again
I Always Win
I Call the Shots
I Could Kill You
I Don't Know You
    Anymore
I Mean Business
I'll Show You
I'm All Yours!
I'm Gonna Take
    You Down
I'm the Boss
I'm Your Best Friend
I'm Your Man/Woman
I'm Your Only Hope
I've Got Your Back
I've Had It!
Just Doing My Job
Just What I Needed
My Angel
My Hero
My Precious Baby
My Way or the Highway

Never Again
Okay, I Can Do This
Shit or Get Off the Pot
Some Things Never
    Change
Stop Diddling around
That Was Then,
    This Is Now
Try Me
We're in This Together
Welcome to My Par-
    lor (Said the Spi-
    der to the Fly)
Well, Well, We
    Meet Again
Well, Well, Well . . .
What Are Friends for?
What I Say Goes
Yeah, Right!
You Ain't Seen Nothin' Yet
You Owe Me
You're Beautiful
You're Going Down
You're in Good
    Hands, Baby
You're More Beautiful
    Than Ever
You're Playing Me
    for a Fool
You're Irrelevant

On companion DVD 2 to this book, you can watch actors demonstrating scene titles. Go to: TimPhillipsStudio.com/dvd.

In your audition, the moment they are waiting to see is the moment that is the reason the scene exists. The producers are waiting on the edge of their seats for you to hit this moment. If you miss it, it's going to cost you the job. This is where your understanding of the writing of the script is relevant. That key to the scene is the same as your title of scene. Often it represents the urgency, or why you're at a crossroads.

In the Robert Duvall film *Get Low,* for example, a young man is offered a job working for a funeral parlor on one condition: He's got to make a sale to the scariest son of a bitch in town. It's his crossroads because he urgently needs this job. He's got a growing family, a wife and a new baby on the way. It's the Depression and there are no other jobs to be had. If the sale doesn't happen, they're going to starve to death. The title of the scene for an actor auditioning for this part could have been "Now or Never."

If you know your title of scene, your universal human dilemma will be so clear that not only will the audience understand exactly what your character is experiencing, but they'll be able to relate to it by association with similar experiences in their own lives.

Define Your Character with a Cliché

A cliché can be an avenue to crafting the body language and speech patterns that define your character. This is such an important topic that I am devoting the whole of Chapter 12, "Physical and Vocal Adjustments," to a broader discussion of it. For now, the point I mean to emphasize is that crafting from a cliché helps you drop into character, so you can trust it will be there for you from the beginning to the end of your audition.

As soon as you get sides for an audition, questions generally arise, like: How am I going to do this? How am I coming across? The cliché can answer these questions in a heartbeat, as the following anecdote demonstrates.

Sherri Snyder had a very successful experience using a cliché to craft her physical adjustments when she was auditioning for a national commercial for DIRECTV. She went through a round of callbacks that involved improvisations between her and a group of other actors. Throughout it all, the director repeatedly told her, "Just keep doing the same thing you're doing and don't change a thing." One major discovery she made was that she could do multiple takes consistently, "Without," in her words, "trying desperately to remember or even think about what I did before." Having established a cliché for her character, it was easy for Sherri to repeat what she'd done the first time out of the gate. This is how the whole process went down.

When Sherri got an email from her agent containing a breakdown the night before the audition, she thought, *What the hell was he thinking?* The character was so different from her natural personality that she was even a little peeved to be sent out for it. Sherri is extremely feminine, a real girly-girl with an Old Hollywood type of glamour. She wears red lipstick and high heels; and normally you won't catch her in a pair of jeans. However, the breakdown described her role as a "butch horse rancher with a strong jaw, and a strong will, and definitely 'playing for the other team.'" The joke of the ad was that her wealthy father has died and disowned her, leaving his entire estate to his blonde bombshell mistress except for a video collection, which goes to his son; the punch line is that the collection has little value since these same films can be watched online. The words that stood out to Sherri had to do with favoritism toward the father's "only son."

Standing in front of her bedroom mirror, wondering how to act masculine and remain truthful to herself, Sherri put on some of her husband's clothing. Right away she thought of a cliché: "Built rough and tough." Finding that idea, the character was so instantly and fully in her body that it enabled her to have fun with her behavior and unleash herself physically. She took a wide stance, put a hand in one pocket, stuck her chin out, and threw back her shoulders. Seeing the effects, she decided, *Tomorrow, I'm going to the audition in character. And I'm going to stay in character the whole time . . . because this is the only way I'm ever going to be able to maintain it!*

The next day, as she was driving to the audition wearing those same clothes, Sherri drove the whole way as if she was "built rough and tough." Even how she was maneuvering the car was a byproduct of this cliché. She got an image in her mind of herself driving a monster truck. Then she began running a macho fantasy that she was driving a jacked-up truck with a pair of testicles hanging down in the back window.

Ninety percent of any audition is appearance. First impressions are so memorable that looking right is half the battle. The funny thing in Sherri's case was that her clothes and stance spoke so clearly about her character that even though the casting office was very busy that day and the room was packed with actors, she wasn't in the reception area for two seconds when a casting assistant waved to her, saying, "DI-RECTV over here." The assistant had recognized immediately that Sherri was the butch horse rancher.

Once inside the audition room, the casting directors loved the persona Sherri embodied. That's when they started throwing different improvs at her. Because she continued coming from the point of view of the cliché, she hit every single one of them on the nose—so much so, in fact, that the casting team laughed and laughed. Afterwards, she marveled, *Gosh, that just came out of me . . . I didn't have any means to plan it because there were no sides at all.*

Remember, usually all you need when you act is one tool that works solidly for the particular role you're doing. You have a number of tools and techniques at your disposal, so the idea when you're crafting is to keep going until you find that one, magical way that liberates you. It could be this, or something else.

The secret of using a cliché is that it has to be yours. Meaningful clichés have behavior attached to them automatically. Your life history has prepared you to embody clichés, which is why images flood the mind when you use them. You don't need to parse them or try to figure out why they are effective. A big part of your job is to get out of the way and let these images and your accompanying impulses flow into your performance. When you find a cliché that defines a character, it will free you up like hers did for Sherri—and, like her, you'll have fun.

Expletives: Labels You Use to Relate to Other Characters

Let's revisit an idea we looked at briefly in Chapter 7: the idea of giving a private, personally meaningful name to the character you're playing against in your scene (in an audition, this character is read by *the reader)*. If you recall, not only do you want to know the facts about who the object of your attention is (perhaps your father, brother, son, husband), but you also want to adopt your character's point of view about this individual. That P.O.V. comes from the history and circumstances the screenwriter provides you.

Through Sherlock Holmesing the text, you discover clues about the relationship. Then, with a special name that stirs you up, you encapsulate how that person makes you feel. It's like a secret code word, if you will, that changes your behavior. Symbolizing the essence of a person with a carefully selected cliché (for example, Captain Doom or Dr. McSteamy) is a powerful way to trigger an immediate, visceral response in your body.

This particular variation on the use of a cliché is a tool that I call an *"expletive."* For sure, it works well as a means of defining the reader. This, of course, goes a long way toward nailing the truth of the first moment of your scene, since you're aiming your lines to the reader. But the expletive is not limited to the person seated directly in front of you. You can also invent expletives that define every person named in the script.

TheFreeDictionary.com defines an expletive as an "exclamation or oath, especially one that is profane, vulgar, or obscene." That sounds derogatory, doesn't it? Or at least crude and rude? Well, keep in mind that human emotions and life aren't as tidy as a tea party. Peasants make great actors because they live in their guts, not in their heads. Think of the great performances you've seen delivered by actors who work from the gut, artists like the late Anne Bancroft, or Philip Seymour

Hoffman and Kathy Bates. Gut. Gut. Gut. Watch their films and you'll see what I mean. If they worried about being polite, they wouldn't be half as interesting on screen.

Watch Kathy Bates' performance in the 2002 film *About Schmidt.* There's a scene where she strips off her clothes and hops into a hot tub naked with Jack Nicholson. She's entirely unapologetic and unashamed, as she aims to seduce him. She's playing the truth of her character in that moment. Bates is fearless and so, so entertaining to watch. Also watch her in her Academy Award-winning role as a psychopath in *Misery* (1990).

For the purpose of acting, an expletive may be a curse word ("Asshole" or "Bitch"), a phrase ("Miss Goody Two Shoes"), or a sound ("Mmm" or "Ick"); and it may be either positive ("Love of my life") or negative ("Schmuck" or "Cunt"). The only caveat here is that your choice needs to be an expletive that makes sense in the context of your scene. The expletive is something you keep to yourself. The casting director won't know what you're thinking exactly, so you can be as obscene in your mind as you like.

Expletives help you take your character's point of view. Because we think in pictures they help us find the right image that causes us to feel. Meeting an IRS agent, the picture is "I'm screwed." Marrying the man of your dreams, the picture is "The greatest day of my life." Hamlet debating suicide, the picture is "To be or not to be." Each picture carries emotion, which draws real body language and sounds out of us—and then it draws forth a picture in the mind of the audience. I asked one student of mine to describe the "hottest chick" he ever went out with, and his response without hesitation was one word, the expletive "Smokin'." His picture gave me a picture. I saw what he meant in my mind's eye.

As an actor you will often have to walk yourself through a deliberate process in order to find the right cliché for a particular scene. Crafting is about building a bridge from you to the character. Put into practice, here's how that can work.

First you look at the facts of the scene. Imagine how it would be for you. Let's say that *your son* caught you cheating on his father (which might happen to a character in a scene for a nighttime soap opera like *Gossip Girl),* how would you feel? That's the kind of life experience and reality you can discover while crafting. Fantasize about your scene until you find that emotional essence. Once you've found it—let's say that, in this case, the truth is you feel *ashamed*—you're beginning to get somewhere.

By personally knowing the essence of the scene, you're one step closer to identifying a powerful expletive that makes sense in the given circumstances.

I worked with an actress in class on this very choice. First, she said, "My son is *my conscience,"* which was accurate, but had no emotion to it. She searched her emotional Rolodex some more. Then she said, "He's *my soul."* Everyone in the room could see her body language changing at this point as she got closer. This expletive was not up in her head; she'd put her hand on her chest when she said it. The son was becoming a pinch for her "ouch." She looked back down at the script in her lap and saw that the playwright had given the answer to her in a line. Finally, she said, "He's *my first love."* As she did, her whole body and tone of voice shifted and brought out the reality of the scene.

My advice is not to work from what the other person "makes" you feel in the moment. Instead, deal with the reality of the relationship and craft your expletives from there; then insert them into the moment. That's why a son wouldn't be a "conscience," but is a "first love." Working off someone you care about is much different from working off of a critic. It changes what you want the person to understand about you. The playwright is sending you down a narrow path. If you walk it with integrity, crafting from the clues you've found in the script, your body can be trusted to respond appropriately.

Rarely is there a character arc within a single scene; most of the time, you'll begin the scene exactly where you end. So once you've found that end point, you can go back to the front of the script and use the expletive to start off strong. This is how to take generality and complexity and reduce it to the simplicity of specificity in a way that's engendered by your gut instincts. You can make choices very quickly when you work in this way.

Though learning to craft clichés may take a bit of time, after a while you'll see that it happens almost simultaneously with hunting for clues on your first reading of the sides.

Building an Inner Dialogue Parallel to the Script

To reduce the complexity of a scene down to its core essence, try coming up with paraphrases that correspond to your character's emotional reality for everything you say and everything you hear. Use a cliché wherever one seems possible. This cliché shouldn't just be a translation of the same meaning into different words, like translating a French sentence *("J'ai faim")* into an English sentence ("I'm hungry.")

Rather, it should represent what's going on inside your character's mind.

For example, an innocuous seeming line, like, "Nice to see you again," said to a business rival (let's label him "Suck up"), might have the cliché "You're going down" behind it. You could jot that cliché in the margin on the page, next to your line.

When the Suck-up rival replies, "Good to see you, too, Bob. Are you joining us at the Club?" your cliché might be "You'd better fuckin' believe it." You could jot that down in the margin of the script beside his dialogue.

Sometimes the cliché for a given line of dialogue you say or hear can be an expletive for a person, a place, a thing, or an event. Other times, it can serve you best to craft parallel dialogue that compresses the essence of your emotional reality. For example, imagine your character is cornered in a scene at a cocktail party by a neighbor who keeps rambling on and on, and in the process doesn't give you an opening to escape. Parallel dialogue might be, "Will you *ever* shut up?" or "Someone save me!"

Parallel dialogue is an excellent way to handle moments in which your character is lying. Of course, you have to decide if your character is a good liar or a poor one. If you see a lie, that's always an important consideration. You could play it straight or you could be obvious. With a cliché you could do it either way.

Parallel dialogue also is useful in establishing menace beneath the lines of a villain or sexual innuendo. A male student brought sides for an audition for a horror movie to class. The role was to play a male co-worker of the lead character, who was an attractive young female scientist at the Centers for Disease Control. From the script we picked up that he was probably the comic relief in the piece, and possibly a future murder victim. He was not identified as a killer. The scene took place in their offices at the end of the day. It involved him asking her out on a date and being turned down. My student said his character was a charming rascal, a press agent rather than a scientist, whose job was to glad-hand drug company officials on the CDC schmooze circuit. His expletive for the scientist was "Ooh Baby," and his title of scene was "Hey There."

The dialogue of the piece was relatively banal, so it was imperative for him to find a way to do the scene that was specific and entertaining on a deeper level—otherwise it would be boring in the extreme. I suggested he amplify the sexual tension by writing parallel dialogue. Every time he identified a word or phrase in the script that could be spun with innuendo, he would paraphrase it as an inner thought his character was having. "Look for any words that imply sex," I said, "and also for words that have to do with the body." Since the scene was about sex, he had to look for places to show it.

In the sides, my student found lines about walking, breathing, and swallowing. To solidify his P.O.V., in the margin on his pages beside where the scientist mentioned swallowing, he wrote down the thought: "You can swallow me anytime, baby!" When we shot him reading the scene, he came alive as a character that reminded everyone in the room of Robert Downey, Jr.'s performance as a playboy in *Iron Man*.

Having parallel dialogue makes you a better listener. It helps you be specific and to play only one thing in the moment. Whatever you come up with, however, must serve the through-line of the scene: Your title of scene helps you hone in on this objective.

Humanizing the Script

Every variation on clichés, from expletives, to the title of scene and parallel dialogue, mainly helps you in your private rehearsal process. For once you find these truthful notes that add up the music of the scene, you have to let go and trust that they will still be there *inside of your body* when you actually go to do your audition. You have to deal with the reality of the moment and remain open to happy accidents as you're performing.

For your rehearsal process, run your inner life by dialoguing with yourself aloud and improvising around your clichés. Talk out loud about your character's dilemma. This is the technique that I call *"humanizing."* Continue humanizing while you're in your car or on the street or in the subway on the way to the audition.

Even though she'd always been very successful in her career, when we worked together Jayne Brook told me that she had never really known what to do on the way to the audition. After she started using humanizing, she told me, "It changed my life." I can't tell you how excited she was.

On companion DVD 2 to this book, watch actors demonstrate the art of humanizing to see and hear what this powerful technique looks like in action prior to a rehearsal. Go to: TimPhillipsStudio.com/dvd.

Once the camera rolls, and even before the director says, "Action," you need to be alive and thoroughly immersed in your situation.

 Notes

----

CHAPTER 10
FIND REASONS TO FEEL

" *Feelings are like a timid animal—if you approach them, they run away. Let them come to you.* "
—Michael Howard

How you feel about any object creates its reality on film. If your relationship to each of the people, places, things, and events in the lines of your script is specific, then, during your audition, you'll get a great result: You'll be like a ball in a pinball machine, hitting against flippers and bumpers, and bouncing off of them in different directions. Your scene will come alive as your body is organically filled with emotions. Most importantly, you'll be engaging to watch on camera. This is the power of *personalization.*

To personalize a script, you simply take the given circumstances the screenwriter has provided to you—facts you discovered while Sherlock Holmesing the script—and give yourself a point of view about them by using an "As If." There are two kinds.

With As Ifs, you can bridge the elements in a particular scene to aspects of your own life. For example, "It's *as if* this character is my brother George." In this way, you are overlaying your thoughts and feelings about your brother onto the scene (love, envy, and so on), lending it reality. This type of substitution works only if you've got a strong P.O.V. about your brother or whatever As If you employ.

You can also craft imaginary As Ifs that stir you up in the way the script demands. For example, "It's *as if* this character is George Clooney." (We're assuming, of course, that this would mean something to you personally *if it were true.)* For you, that meaning might be: "It's *as if* he's the sexiest (or most suave) man in the world." And then you overlay the meaning on the context of the scene: rejection, seduction, and so on.

No matter what substitution you choose for a person, place, thing, or event, your crafting must involve daydreaming around it in the context of the scene you're doing so that it comes alive for you. Pictures are not real until you attach an emotion to them. Pictures and sensations just drop in or pop up, and emotions arise of their own accord when you find an As If that works. You can trust these. An actor's first impulse is usually dead-on. It is in trying to improve that first impulse where actors often go wrong.

Here's a key thing to remember about the technique of personalization. For As Ifs, or substitutions, to work in your favor, you must begin by knowing what kind of emotion is wanted in the scene (anger, sorrow, elation, remorse, and so on). This is not arbitrary. It's dictated to you by the script. From there, you can work toward generating it.

The rehearsal process is something like this. You find your character's point of view. Let's say your character arrives for a business meeting with a man he views as a "sneaky bastard." The script says that you shake hands. As an actor, you must ask yourself: "How would I shake hands with a 'sneaky bastard?'" Maybe you do it "*as if* he's Bernie Madoff" and you imagine that's "*as if* he's got a slimy hand that makes yours wet." The second As If is the personalization of an object: in this case, the sneaky bastard's hand. This is how layers of substitution can factor into the moments in the script.

The personalization comes from knowing what the substitution means to you. You know you *despise* Bernie Madoff. You know that shaking a wet hand is *creepy.*

You don't need to worry or fuss too much about how to create layered responses, as you're already a layered person. That's why specific As Ifs work. Your choices will read. As I like to say in my classes: You don't need to act if you know who the bitch is.

When Roma Maffia was in my class in the '90s, she brought in her scenes for the role of Michael Douglas's lawyer in *Disclosure.* When she found her As If, "It's as if I am an arrow," she found the physical life of her character. It was her first major role in a film and she was able to more than hold her own in scenes with Demi Moore and Douglas.

Personalization can help you shift your state of being—even turning your emotions on a dime—without pushing for a result. As we'll discuss, it's an effective approach to crafting the entire moment-by-moment reality of a longer scene, or just to bring a specific moment to its fullest potential. I can't tell you how often I'm asked, "What do I do with one line?" My reply to this question is to use this tool. It's a great way to deliver a crystal clear performance and full-blown reality in a one- or two-line audition.

The Three Parts of Crafting Relationships That Make You Feel

Owning the moment as an actor means finding a reason for you to believe in, and genuinely associate with how your character is feeling. An event happens (a line is said or an action taken). There is how you feel about. Then it calls forth an image within you. This last part of the relationship to the script happens after you identify the feeling.

The funny thing about it, as you'll soon discover, is that in practice this process is happening in nanoseconds inside your body. Thoughts and emotions prompt each other to arise. Your job is to sort through them and make selections that serve the script.

As you rehearse with your sides in hand, each time you come to a line about, or a description of, a person, an object, a place, or an event, stop and take steps to personalize it. Once you find a reason to care, create an image of what you are seeing. The body will remember this image if you give it to yourself, and then, every time you reach that line in the scene, its meaning will come flooding back to you effortlessly.

After personalizing the first person/place/thing/event, go back and re-read the script from the beginning and keep going until you hit the next thing you need to personalize. Take those same steps again: find a reason to care and compose an image. Then go back to the beginning, start again, and go on down until you hit the third.

If you find and craft twenty relationships in this manner, before you're finished rehearsing the sides you'll have gone through them twenty times and you'll practically be off book by then.

On companion DVD 2 to this book, you will see how personalization helps with lines. Visit TimPhillipsStudio.com/dvd.

You're not required to memorize the sides for an audition, of course, and I advocate holding the script no matter what, but having a high degree of familiarity with the sides is useful when it comes naturally out of the crafting process.

It is far too easy to go to the level of the story instead of crafting. It is too easy to imagine the other character's point of view and become engaged with it. To avoid this acting trap and stay in your own P.O.V. you must use your own images, those that arise in response to your feelings. This is an abstract and impressionistic way of working. But you can trust it. Generate the emotion first. Then let your muscle memory provide you with an image. That emotion gives your image meaning. The anchor of memory is emotion.

Great moments in scenes are often accidental. They happen in a performance as a result of having crafted the history of a relationship to a person, place, thing, or event, and then being surprised at what happens in you when the history comes up as you're performing the dialogue. An emotional response is just there, like a kneejerk reaction. The history you've crafted provokes it.

Relationships to People

The first relationship you need to develop in any scene is your relationship to your scene partner. In an audition setting, this person is the reader. As we discussed in Part One, the reader is primary to you because he or she is present and feeding you lines. Also if you personalize this relationship first it will help you deliver a great first moment. In the last chapter, we discussed how useful clichés are for establishing your life in the first moment. Daydreaming to personalize your relationship with the reader (including any history and expectations you might have of him/her) adds another layer there.

In Chapter 7, we briefly explored the technique of labeling the reader: coming up with a name that's shorthand for how you feel about him or her. This was part of how you discovered *what you wanted that person to understand about you*. Here we're doing something a little bit different, but you'll find that it fits with the objective you found.

Let's say your line of dialogue is: "I have never seen Harriet looking better." What do you do with that? First, you ask, "What did the screenwriter imply my character feels?" Because you've Sherlock Holmesed the text, you know the answer: turned on.

Next, you generate the feeling of "turned on" in your body. Your body knows this and other feelings from past experience. Your whole life has been preparation for this.

Then, you run some mental film footage of what you are saying: Let's say you see yourself walking towards Harriet at a party. Since you say, "I never saw her looking better," you know you've seen her before. How can you own that line—believe in it? Here's where an improvisation comes in handy. Recall (in your imagination) those earlier times when Harriet looked hot and it turned you on. Back in tenth grade you thought she was hot, so you asked her out and she laughed at you. Here you are ten years later at the party, and you're looking at her, and thinking, *Wow, I am going to hit on her again!*

154

Having given yourself these memories through fantasizing about them, you've literally had a life with Harriet. You created an emotional experience, which is a kind of historical knowledge. And guess what? You betcha! The camera sees what you know.

There's a difference between improvisation and visualization that should be pointed out at this juncture. Improvisation is an experience because you say things out loud while you're doing it. Visualization, on the other hand, is a thought. Thought alone is not experience and the body doesn't respond to it as such.

Do you doubt this? It's the difference between looking into the baby blue eyes of your significant other and *thinking,* "Boy, do I love her," and actually *saying it aloud.* You can think it and nothing much will happen. Whereas if you say it out loud, your life changes. Your body knows the distinction. With improvisation, you must speak aloud.

Relationships to Objects

If you want to see a perfect example of an actor who has crafted a strong relationship to an object, watch Anthony Hopkins in *The Remains of the Day.* In this 1993 Merchant-Ivory costume drama, Hopkins plays an elderly butler reminiscing several years later on his service in the household of a wealthy British lord prior to World War Two. Loyal, calm, and efficient, he runs the household in a traditional manner, as if the staff were invisible. He is intimate with no one. When the less reserved housekeeper (played by Emma Thompson) visits him in the privacy of his study, she casually reaches out for the novella that he's been reading and he pulls the book back toward his body. In this one gesture, it becomes evident that there's an emotional line the butler is unwilling to cross.

I've heard that Hopkins isolated himself off set prior to shooting this scene. Whatever particular meaning he assigned to the book was so emotionally devastating to him that it left him sobbing and drained. The director and crew had to hold the shot for twenty minutes while he composed himself to do the take. Then he did not need to do several takes of the scene; they shot it in one. That's how powerful the relationship with an object can be. If you can specifically craft a moment for an audition that's as compelling as this one, you can be sure it will be a moment that impresses the casting director and creative team.

Objects are often symbols of a character's history. In a recent film study class, a student brought in a scene to work on that was taken from the 1994 film *Quiz Show*. Her role was Toby Stempel, the wife of a contestant who was winning tons of money on *Twenty One*, a 1950's TV quiz show that was rigged by the producers. In this particular scene (which was played between Johann Carlo and John Turturro in the movie), my student was working across from a reader doing the lines of her husband. The underlying reality of the moment is that Toby, who is a working-class woman, is afraid that her husband will leave her now that he has made so much money. That's the subtext. On the surface, the lines are merely an argument about a suit.

The suit needs to be dry-cleaned.

"Why does this matter to Toby?" I asked. "What is the couple's relationship to this suit? What is the screenwriter implying that Toby feels about her father? And what is the screenwriter implying that she should feel about her husband's treatment of the suit?" In this case, we decided the emotion being called for was *disappointment.* We determined from the script that her father had bought the suit. (She loves him.) Now her husband wears the suit (a symbol for their marriage), but from her P.O.V. he's not taking proper care of it. As you can imagine, this raised the stakes for the actress playing the scene.

By personalizing the suit by giving herself some memories of her father wearing it, and knowing what he meant to her, she quickly came to life in front of our eyes.

Relationships to Places

In writer Aaron Sorkin's 1992 film *A Few Good Men,* Jack Nicholson's character, Colonel Nathan R. Jessep, runs the U.S. military base in Guantanamo Bay, Cuba. The location of that base standing in a "hot" zone between America and hostile Russian-backed Cuban forces is of enormous significance to the plot. This is made clear when Jessep says he does his job to protect America so that others don't have to. He makes it clear that his location entitles him to do as he sees fit on the base, including ordering the murder of a marine who wasn't good at his job. He views himself as above the law, indicating that it doesn't apply to men like him; he should be thanked and not questioned.

Not only did Nicholson need to personalize the base for himself, I believe every other actor on the film needed to personalize its meaning. It's essentially a silent character in the film, one whose presence is felt everywhere.

If you get handed a script with a title like *A Year in Tuscany* or *My Life as a House,* asking yourself questions about how the location factors into your scenes is a very good idea. Does your scene take place in a church? A casino? A courtroom? A hospital? What your location means to your character in the moment your scene takes place is something to make a specific choice about, and do some daydreaming on, because this can help you establish history. It is human nature to relate to our surroundings.

Places can be symbolic of people. Writers recognize this fact. The meaning of place is used to full advantage in the play *All My Sons* by Arthur Miller, in which two sons went to war and only the younger one came home. It was shot for television and aired on PBS in 1987 with Aidan Quinn playing the surviving son. He has a powerful scene in the backyard of the family home, in which his character wants to kiss the girl his brother intended to marry. They are standing in front of a tree that was struck by lightning. He's in love with her and wants to ask her to marry him, but he can't do it there because the tree and the backyard remind him of his dead brother. Any actor who plays this role must find a way to imaginatively personalize the tree and the yard.

Furthermore, any place that's mentioned in a script, such as in a line of dialogue like, "Do you remember how it was when we went to Jamaica?" can be personalized. Bridge that place to your own life with an As If and allow yourself to recall an image of it.

Relationships to Events

Let's say you have a line, such as, "What the fuck did you do twenty years ago—put a gun to his head in the desert, then shoot him?" Well, that's a very specific picture you can act. You can generate a feeling about this man being shot in the desert, based on your character's point of view. Simply daydream about the event being described in the line and substituting As Ifs for the man who was shot, for the shooter, and perhaps for what you did in the period following the man's disappearance. Once you have a picture in your mind of the event that gets your emotional motor running, let it remain true for you until the other character in the scene denies it. Then the picture can change.

A screenwriter suggests experiences and an actor translates those suggestions into emotionally generated reality. In acting, there are really only four or five emotions. Not hundreds. Don't get complicated for film and television. There's no time for that. In your general homework you give yourself to improve your acting, spend time daydreaming about the things that produce genuine emotional responses in you. Then, when you need them, they'll be there for you to supply to the sides you're given as appropriate. You can increase your ability to access your emotions. Become like a well-oiled machine.

A Few Notes about Working with Your Imagination

Good actors are students of human nature. As an actor, you should be collecting As Ifs from your own life, and also from the world around you. Make up stories about the people you see on the subway or on a bus. Practice describing what you see using As Ifs and studying the body language that goes along with it. For example: It's *as if* the man across from you has lost everything he owned. It's *as if* the woman across from you is having the happiest day of her life. It's *as if* the man you see is a bear . . . or a penguin.

The emotional core of your character will be given to you by the screenwriter, and you're going to need to demonstrate those qualities behaviorally. As Ifs are a shortcut. Stephanie Gunning, my writer, was once cast in an independent film for a supporting character known only as the Depressed Woman. She did her audition for the director as if she was a wet dog waiting in the rain for her master to come back. She didn't move her arms (because dogs don't have arms), but let them hang heavily at her sides. And she imagined the unpleasant sensation of water pouring down and plastering her hair against her head, knowing there was nothing to do about it. The feeling was *abandonment.* She got to this way of doing her audition by asking herself what depression looked like. The image that popped into her mind right away was the wet dog. She never second-guessed it. In rehearsing for the audition, she created a muscle memory of the experience.

When you look for an As If, grab hold of the first images that come to mind. You can trust these because your instant creativity is the purest; it's closest to the core of your life experience. Some people have trouble working imaginatively because their minds get in the way. The mind rationalizes and tries to justify impulses, which can dilute them. Nonetheless subconscious imagery is powerful. It comes from deep inside the body.

Here's an example from a time when I worked with an actress on the role of May in the play *Fool for Love* by Sam Shepard, focusing on a scene in which May recalls walking with her mother to look for her father. She talks about coming across a house and looking through the window, and seeing the other family that her father had inside. He had another wife and a son, and she and her mother watched them all having dinner together. The problem for my student was that the father did not seem real to her in the scene. She didn't believe in what she was saying yet.

"What does the playwright imply you feel about the father sitting there at the table eating chicken with a woman and a kid who is not you?" I asked her. "Is it sadness? Is it anger?" Then I suggested, "Generate that emotion a little, and just let an image come to you." A second later she experienced an involuntary body shudder, like when it's very cold out and you begin shivering. Because the reaction was so immediate and dramatic, I felt I had to ask her, though I rarely do, "What image came to you?"

She replied, "Pizza . . . But I can't figure out the reason."

My advice to her was not to try parsing the image. Knowing "why" doesn't help an actor. What would help her was having the memory of the shudder. That image was stored in her muscle memory. There would be reality for her now in the scene because she had an actual experience to recall. She didn't have to work on it. She could trust it. I also told her that the shiver might or might not happen again. She could let it go and be spontaneous with whatever honestly came up when she performed the play.

Personalizing the Other Actor's Lines

Whenever the other character in your scene expresses a point of view, you can also personalize that line by translating what you're hearing into your own P.O.V. For instance, if the other makes an accusation, such as, "You are such a lowlife, dishonorable bastard for cheating on your wife," in the margin of your script you might write, "I'm better than that!" In that moment, you're being insulted. The reality of the moment comes from revealing how you feel about it. Even if you don't say a word, during an audition the camera will be shooting a close-up on your face as you're listening to those lines. Ask yourself: What would that moment be like for you? Don't try to act the story, the entire plot of the script. Just act that one moment by personalizing it. It's *as if* . . .

All really great acting happens when an actor is not talking. It occurs when the actor cannot talk, but there's clearly been a "pinch" and the actor is feeling an "ouch." The camera loves those moments because the audience sees the scene reflected through the character's eyes. Think back on scenes you've watched on TV where someone is staring horrified at a brutal murder scene or the twisted remnants of a catastrophic car crash. You didn't need to see a dead body yourself, because you saw it in the actor's response.

What Do You Do with One Line?

You can build the history of a character around a single line of dialogue by crafting a specific As If for the person who you're saying that line to, and by daydreaming a specific memory (or memories) of your history together. My student James DuMont did this when he auditioned for the role of a pizza parlor manager in the 2011 black comedy, *Killer Joe.* One of the lead actors, Gina Gershon, plays a waitress who is hatching a plot with her brother to murder their mother. In the sides James read from, the description said that the manager "lurks in the background" watching while the uniformed waitress, Sharla, talks on the phone. Then he tells her to get off the line. Not much to go on for an actor—or was it enough? We worked together on his preparation for this audition.

We began by looking at how he could personalize the waitress: Who was she to him? In the stage directions it said that the waitress keeps moving away from the manager. We knew she would be sexy, because Gina Gershon specializes in playing seductive women. We also knew her character was "white trash" because of her name: Sharla. In addition, we knew that he doesn't fire her, even though she talks on the telephone at work, which is against the rules, as the line he was given about "no personal calls" made clear.

How could those clues we found through Sherlock Holmesing be added up? In our coaching session, James decided that they implied she was "hot" and he "wanted her." That's the reason he would let her improper workplace behavior slide. That the script described him as lurking was a creepy choice of words, so he must be a "creepy" guy.

I coached James by asking him, "How many times has he told her no personal calls?" To heighten the meaning of his line and create a history behind it, he decided that they'd had the same conversation about no calls being allowed on duty many times before.

Even though it was a one-line scene for him, he needed to find a turning point for his character. "Why does this scene take place for his character?" Right before the manager speaks to the waitress, the script says that she laughs. I advised James to craft his impulse to approach Sharla and to say his line on the sound of her laughter. From there James put in his creative filler through daydreaming. In that way, he personalized his audition.

It's worth mentioning that although James did not get cast for this particular part, since he's been using this approach to his auditions his career has really begun to take off. In the last two years, he's made twenty movies, and he shot a recurring role as the character of Bill in five episodes of the second season of the TNT series *Men of a Certain Age*. It just proves my point: You must audition for your career, not the job.

These steps are an example of how you can make a viable scene from few details. You can use even one or two lines to reveal the truth of any human being. As an actor in film and television, your victories come from your moments themselves, not from the film as a whole. You won't hear the applause of an audience. Your reward is in the satisfaction of doing excellent work. Making specific choices in an audition that read truthfully on camera about the moments in your scenes that are related to people, things, places, and events is a victory you can celebrate no matter whether you are cast or not.

 Notes

----

Notes

- -

- -

- -

- -

- -

- -

- -

- -

- -

- -

- -

- -

- -

- -

- -

- -

CHAPTER 11

DEFINE YOUR SOCIAL DICTATE

> " *The actor cannot afford to look only to his own life for all his material, nor pull strictly from his own experience to find his acting choices and feelings.* "
> —**Stella Adler**

In prepping for an audition in a hurry, you should always be on the alert for shortcuts that can give you specific moments. This isn't rocket science. You just need to have a steady stream of life flowing through your mind that reads well on camera: clear, precise, and accurate knowledge. A tool called the *social dictate* can serve you in this capacity.

A social dictate is a physical adjustment that you supply for your character, one directly related to his or her profession or social standing—and, in dramatic situations, it will *always* be a source of conflict. An aspect of the situation will demand that the character fight against this rule. Take, for example, the 1997 film *Good Will Hunting,* about a twenty-year old janitor at M.I.T. named Will (played by Matt Damon) who is a mathematical genius with an eidetic memory. Damon and

Ben Affleck won an Oscar for Best Screenplay for writing the film's script. A product of foster care and the juvenile detention system, Will has suffered abuse and is angry. He often gets in fights and has been arrested. A judge has released him to supervision by a professor who recognizes his talent and on the condition that he goes into therapy. Against his will, he begins going to see a psychologist named Sean Maguire (played by Robin Williams). A game ensues between them where Will uses all of his intelligence to manipulate Sean and find a point of weakness that he can use to his advantage to throw Sean off balance.

In an early scene, where Sean does his best to gain Will's trust, Robin Williams adheres to the social dictate of being calm, rational, conversational, and available to his client. He is seated in a chair, smiling kindly, his body language is open, and he therefore sends out the clear message, "I'm listening. I'm watching you objectively. I care about you. I'm no threat to you." For his part, Will moves around the room commenting on its contents. He fixates upon a paint-by-numbers painting of a tiny ship being tossed in a storm. He knows it is symbolic and uses the opportunity to press in on Sean to see if he'll open a crack. He says, 'Maybe you're one step away from cutting off your own ear," like Vincent Van Gogh. He guesses Sean's wife left him and that Sean was devastated.

There is a line upon which we can see Sean warning Will that he's about to overstep. The truth is that Sean's wife died of cancer and he has not yet recovered from the loss. This is a central theme defining the character of Sean, which later factors into the main lesson he teaches Will. But Will ignores the warning and continues making guesses. He insults Sean's wife. In a flash, Sean crosses the room and pushes Will up against the wall holding him by the throat. He says, "If you disrespect my wife again, I will end you."

When you see such a line, as an actor, recognize that it is the "money shot," the moment the producers are looking to capture on film, the one where the character struggles to maintain his dictate or abandons it altogether. It should be clear to you that the social dictate in operation for your character is in conflict with that line expressing your character's values. It's a moment of intense emotion. Emotion generates reality.

Maybe your character will be going back and forth between two polarities on different lines in a particular scene. The social dictate can help set up those contrasts.

What Is a Social Dictate?

Let me give you a brief definition. A social dictate is a law imposed upon you by those of your own kind, club, or ilk. As such, it's an emblem of character, a motto, a slogan, or an internal badge that you wear and embody. For example:

- *The army:* "Be all that you can be."
- *The marines:* "The few, the proud."
- *The police:* "Serve and protect."
- *A judge:* "This is my room" or "Not in my room."
- *A therapist:* "I am available" or "I'm listening."
- *A doctor:* "We did the best we could" or "We will do the best we can."
- *A nurse:* "I'm doing all I can do."
- *A detective:* "One step ahead of you."

- *A waitress:* "Hurry up and order, 'cuz my 'dogs are barking.'"
- *A politician's wife:* "Stand by your man."
- *A litigator:* "Any reasonable person would come to the same conclusion."

On companion DVD 2 to this book, you can see a demonstration of a social dictate. Notice how the social dictate changes the actor's body language. Go to: TimPhillipsStudio.com/dvd.

Once you have identified this stock phrase defining the main expectation imposed on your character's behavior by his or her social peers, what do you do with it? You will craft an expression of it through a physical adjustment that the camera picks up, as that is how the audience can read it. The social dictate is perceived through your body language and your eyes. The physical adjustment makes you seem to be who you are. If you were playing Sean Maguire in *Good Will Hunting,* this means you might lean backwards in your chair with your arms open or perhaps sit still with your hands clasped and your head tilted to express your therapist social dictate: availability and intent listening.

Look at the physical life of other therapist roles in movies and on TV and you'll see how those actors and actresses embody a similar dictate as Williams does in *Good Will Hunting.* There's Gabriel Byrne from *In Treatment,* playing Paul, a psychotherapist who spends major portions of every episode seated in a chair listening to his patients. There's Lorraine Bracco, playing Dr. Jennifer Melfi, in *The Sopranos,* where she must walk a tight line of therapeutic neutrality while counseling a murderous mob boss.

There's also Alan Arkin, portraying Dr. Oatman in the 1997 comedy *Grosse Point Blank,* who's an anomaly in this category. The first time we see him on screen, Oatman is already feeling so threatened by the hit man (played by John Cusack) who's been coming to see him that he is trying to fire him, explaining that he does not want to be emotionally involved in his patients' lives. The more rational he appears to be in his refusal, the bigger the conflict the situation imposes upon Oatman—and this, of course, makes his struggle to maintain composure extremely funny to watch. Arkin leans forward and holds his head. His body language shows he's a frightened, defeated therapist.

Part of the beauty of the social dictate is that they are recyclable. You can use them again and again for roles in different projects, as well as to craft specific moments that occur in different scenes in the same project. Guest stars are like snow ploughs, as they are used to push the plot of a piece forward. Unless you are auditioning for the lead in the show, you can rest assured that you are there, on the project, to serve the lead characters and plot. Understanding your character's social dictate helps you to fulfill this purpose.

Just remember that there has to be a reason for your character to act in whatever way you settle upon. You can play one or the other bits of crafting in a given moment. Be specific in your choices. Expressing a social dictate does not mean imitating someone's physical behavior. You have to find the reason for the behavior. Know the reason. This knowledge will read on camera.

A social dictate is like the words on the plaque under a statue in a museum. What should your plaque read on a specific line? Try out several phrases during your crafting process. Keep at it until you find one that brings your body alive. That's how you know you found the right one. Then, rehearse the social dictate, saying it aloud.

There are two types of social dictates: those of subculture, such as the ones we've just been considering, and those of period. Let's look more closely at how to craft them from the numerous clues you've Sherlock Holmesed from your script.

Defining Your Social Dictate

An actress came to my workshop with sides to work on drawn from the script of the 2003 film *Cold Mountain,* which was adapted by Anthony Minghella (who also directed the film) from the 1997 National Book Award-winning novel of the same name by Charles Frazier. The action is set in the rural South of the Confederacy during the American Civil War. For practice, my student intended to read for Ruby Thewes, the part Renée Zellweger played, for which she won an Oscar for Best Actress in a Supporting Role. Basically, Ruby is a dirt-poor farmer who has been scraping out an existence doing physical labor. In her first scene, she arrives at the farm of Ada Monroe (played in the film by Nicole Kidman), a minister's daughter raised in the city, who is struggling to survive on her own now that the men have left town. Ruby needs this job for her survival, and, in her manner, she's negotiating a contract between them. She knows she has to prove to Ada that she can do the job.

Ruby's first line was, "Here I am." Not much happened on her first camera take. So I guided her to identify a social dictate that would affect her body, and in the process also help her identify a source of potential conflict in the script. Did it come from being a woman? Did it from being in the South? Did it come from being poor? Those were questions my student needed to answer. We came up with the social dictate, "I 'git' the job done." That was what she wanted Ada to understand.

Now when my student said her line on her next camera take, as she said it she put her hands on her hips with a blunt demeanor. It gave her truthful body language. Upon seeing this, I told the entire class, "Avoid logic at all costs. You always know who a person is by what they do, not what they say. The phrase you choose for the social dictate doesn't have to mean anything to anyone else but you. It's a phrase that brings you to life."

The ground rule for using a social dictate is that it must be in conflict with the circumstances in which you find yourself. The Civil War took place in the 1860s. For a costume drama, necessarily as an actor you will look for a social dictate. Every era going backward from the decade before your current decade is a period piece. For an actor in 2012, that means anything prior to the years around the turn of the millennium. You can find a rule for any era. For instance, the 1980's rule would be: "Where's my money?"

Here's the way to find your most relevant social dictate. First write down the facts you have about your character—just the stone cold facts with no elaboration or interpretation put on them. No story. For a woman, the first thing she should write down is: Woman/girl. Then: and/or daughter/sister/mother. For a man, the first thing he should write down is: Man/boy. Then: and/or brother/son/father.

Keep going down the line of facts—your given circumstances—from there.

Once you have all the facts on a piece of paper, you will go down the list and look for conflict in the scene you are playing. Which fact on the list of facts is the source of the character's conflict?

We know from the sides of *Cold Mountain* that Ruby arrives single, barefoot, and feral. She looks as if she was raised in a barn. Which fact is the central source of conflict in this script? Is Ruby's conflict based in her womanhood? Is it in her daughterhood? Is it in her motherhood? I can think of movies where those would have been the right answers.

In *Victor/Victoria,* the conflict for the lead (Julie Andrews) came from being a woman.

In *The Heiress,* the conflict for the lead (Olivia de Havilland) came from being a daughter.

In *Crazy Heart,* the conflict for the lead character's girlfriend (Maggie Gyllenhaal) came from being a mother.

For Ruby, in this scene where Ada and Ruby meet, her inherent conflict is based in being a poor woman. She has urgency and stands at a crossroads: She desperately needs this job. Unless she persuades Ada to hire her, she'll be homeless and hungry. A lower-class woman in the 1860s has a certain place in the world. She must work to survive and be willing to get her hands dirty. But she normally wouldn't be hired to replace a man. Here, because the men in town have gone to war, she has a shot at a job doing hard manual labor, but only if Ada comes to understand that Ruby "can do the job as well as any man could."

Economic class is a source of conflict for Eliza Doolittle (Audrey Hepburn) in *My Fair Lady*, where she is dictated before her transformation to "mind your manners" or "know your place." Before her first bath, Eliza keeps repeating, "I'm a good girl, I am," meaning that she's not a prostitute.

There are actually two social dictates in that film: the before and the after. As a destitute flower girl, living in the gutter, she must "be tough to survive," though there are clearly certain things Eliza will not do because of her character as a "good girl." Once she becomes a lady, her social dictate changes to "I must be a proper lady at all times."

Once you have your social dictate, you can rehearse it by saying it aloud to yourself at the beginning of the scene. "A good lower-class woman must always know her place." Then go on and say your line. See what kind of life flows out of you . . . Are you defying the social dictate already? "Here I am," says Ruby, issuing a challenge to Ada.

The Social Dictate as a Plot Twist

Here's a gender dictate that comes from the same period as *Cold Mountain*. It's used as a plot twist in Mark Twain's novel *The Adventures of Huckleberry Finn*. Huck is impersonating a girl. He's wearing a dress. Someone suspecting him tosses a ball at him and he catches it between his knees. His disguise is penetrated. Boys have to catch that way because they wear pants. But a girl from the same era would naturally do the opposite: She would open her knees and let the fabric of her dress serve her like a baseball catcher's mitt.

There is a scene in Quentin Tarantino's 2009 film *Inglourious Basterds* where social behavior is used to penetrate a disguise, thus heightening the dramatic tension and furthering the plot in a certain direction. This social dictate has to do with nationality. A group of British and American soldiers are undercover in a German bar, where they have come disguised as German soldiers to meet a contact in the Resistance—a well-known actress. At a nearby table, an officer takes notice of them and decides to test their credibility. He provokes one of them to order three beers, which the man does by holding up three open fingers: the first, middle, and ring fingers. At which point the German officer shoots him dead.

Why? How did the German officer know the man he shot was not who he said he was? Because Germans typically indicate the number three by holding up thumb, the first finger, and the middle finger. Failing to follow social conventions revealed the lie.

Fortunately, this important point was explained in the script. The facts you will need are always and only in your script. Using that as your guide, give yourself a motto or an axiom for your character to live by. Once you know your character's inherent conflict, your lines will sound different to you. They'll be more resonant, specific, and playable. You will also hear other people's lines differently.

Crafting moments off of social dictates can be loads of fun. Before your auditions, you can spend time improvising around them. You can also practice them at home in front of a camera to study their impact on your body language— both your natural physical responses and specific choices you make. In the next chapter we'll discuss in detail how character can be revealed through crafted physical adjustments.

 Notes

----

Notes

CHAPTER 12
PHYSICAL AND VOCAL ADJUSTMENTS

> *Acting is all about honesty. If you can fake that, you've got it made."*
> **—George Burns**

Personality, or *character,* is always expressed through physical adjustments: body language and costumes. Upon occasion it is also expressed through vocal adjustments: an accent, a lisp, a stutter, and so forth. Portraying the meaningful distinctions of a particular character can therefore be as easy as donning a pair of eyeglasses, like Superman does when he wants to become the "mild-mannered" reporter Clark Kent. Or it can come through a decision to smile or scowl, to talk slowly or rapidly, or to sit up straight or slouch when seated. The point is, by embodying a few mannerisms that reveal your character's truth you can drastically change the viewers' perception of you.

Look at the Emmy Award-winning work of Toni Collette who plays the lead role in *United States of Tara* (Showtime).

Playing the series' eponymous heroine, Tara Gregson (a suburban housewife suffering from dissociative identity disorder), she effectively manages to portray several eccentric alternate personalities—or *alters*—using specific physical and vocal adjustments. Tara's personalities include a flirtatious teenager named T; a stereotypical 1950's housewife named Alice; a loud-mouthed, male Vietnam veteran named Buck; an animalistic, id-like creature named Gimme; a Jewish, New York psychotherapist, Shoshana Shoenbaum; and a childish personality named Chicken. There is never any confusion about which alter is present in a scene because Collette's choice as to how to depict each different personality is so specific.

How does Toni Collette make her transformations so believable? Well, for one thing, the audience is in on the joke. It's been explained. For another, everyone in the series accepts that Tara has shifted. Her immediate family relates to Tara's different identities as individuals. Not least, Collette so fully commits to the physical and vocal adjustments she has developed for each alter personality that when the audience sees her, they can guess which one she's playing, and it's fun to watch her rotate among them.

Let's look at exactly what Collette does physically and vocally to make us recognize and believe in the reality of her different alter personalities.

- T typically wears her hair on the top of her head in a slightly off-kilter ponytail tied up with a scrunchie. She has on large hoop earrings, bright lipstick, and obvious eye makeup. Her clothes are provocative. She chews gum with her mouth open while talking— loudly. All her gestures are large. She rolls her eyes and makes faces when she doesn't like what she hears.

180

- Buck wears jeans and cut-off muscle tee-shirts, a leather jacket, a baseball cap, and wire-rimmed glasses. He's a macho man who swaggers and curses. He rarely, if ever, smiles. He has a Southern accent.

- Alice's hair might be neatly coiffed in pin curls and with a scarf holding it in place, resembling Lucille Ball from *I Love Lucy*. Or she could adopt a tone reminiscent of the gentle, yet authoritative mother from *Leave It to Beaver*. She wears ladylike housedresses to do household chores, matching sweater sets, a pearl necklace, and never wears pants. She's the epitome of the traditional housewife of yesteryear.

- Shoshana Shoenbaum could be modeled after the feminist Gloria Steinem as she was in the '70s. She's "modern," keeping her long hair down and wearing rose-tinted eyewear. Her clothes are free flowing and urban sophisticated. She has a New York accent.

- Gimme wears a red poncho and scampers around like a small woodland creature, crouched low to the ground. Gimme doesn't speak, but screams, and it doesn't come out when someone might see it.

- Chicken has the body language of a five-year-old girl.

While we don't know the exact process Toni Collette used internally to craft the personas she plays, she's so good at morphing that it's certain she has made some strong choices. She's found her way of doing each of her characters so that she comes across not as one woman who's pretending to be other people, but literally as seven people.

A trap for a less talented actor in her position would be to try to play the plotline. Rather, the actor needs to ask the same questions on behalf of these seven characters in their scenes that any other actor would ask on behalf of one character. The plot is created by how the scenes are edited together. And this is not an actor's responsibility.

The Way of Doing a Role

One way many actors begin to find meaningful adjustments for their characters is to come up with a metaphor that defines the character's overall through-line. This is an As If. For example, Dustin Hoffman said that he played Willy Loman in the 1985 television production of *Death of a Salesman* as if he was a flea on a hot griddle. His choices came out of that. He won an Emmy for his performance as Willy.

Character adjustments are a byproduct of finding an overarching way of doing a role. Anthony Hopkins played cannibalistic serial killer Hannibal Lecter in *The Silence of the Lambs* (1991) as if he was HAL 9000, the computer, from the 1968 movie *2001: A Space Odyssey.* His voice was calm, steady, and often sarcastic in tone. Like HAL, his character was playing a mental game of control. He won an Oscar for his performance.

In the 1989 film *My Left Foot,* Daniel Day-Lewis played spastic, quadriplegic Irish playwright Christy Brown, a man with only one functional limb. He revealed that as he was crawling around on the floor he saw himself as a fully loaded 747 trying to get off the ground. Like Hopkins, he also won an Academy Award for his portrayal.

When I did a role as a seaman in *The Lightship* in 1985, Robert Duvall played an escaped convict named Mr. Caspary, who was a Southern gentleman and criminal mastermind leading a small gang that hijacked the ship. He told me that his character choice was, "It's as if I'm Tennessee Williams and Truman Capote in the same shoes." In fact, I was with him when he bought the actual shoes he wore for the role in Chinatown in Manhattan. He always likes to find the way his character walks and stands as he develops his physical adjustments for a part. The shoes and how they slide across the floor, for example, can help him find the way the character moves. He was irritated when a well-meaning costumer put rubber soles on Mr. Caspary's shoes thinking she would help Duvall by making sure he wouldn't slip on the deck of the ship where we were filming in the North Sea. But if Mr. Caspary would have slipped, Bob wanted to slip!

The human mind conceives in pictures. For those pictures to be meaningful to an audience they must be translated through the medium of the actor's body and voice. Finding *a way of doing a role* is a first step in making a range of other choices.

Physical, Mental, and Emotional Conditions

Watch Christian Bale in his Academy Award-winning performance as real-life crack-addicted boxer Dicky Eklund in the 2010 film *The Fighter*. He changed his appearance considerably by losing a lot of weight before filming and thinning his hair. He also worked with a vocal coach to develop a Lowell, Massachusetts, dialect. His physicalization of Dicky included a slouch and a wide-eyed stare, unkempt hair, as well as active face making and fidgeting with his body. When he's seated in certain scenes, his knees bounce open and closed, up and down. He had to appear high in many scenes, and did so by working with an adjustment around his mouth and lips (he mushed them around), and his jaw was in almost constant motion, waggling from side to side.

Later in the film, when Dicky has sobered up, Bale stands straighter. His hair is neatly combed. His eyes and face seem relaxed and more still. Through the adjustments he chose for earlier and later scenes, we understand his condition as either strung out or clean. What he never changes, however, is the body language of a boxer that's fundamental to Dicky.

When you're crafting adjustments, the kinds of clues we covered in Chapter 6, "Who Am I?" must be the foundation of your choices. Depending on the script, you could get some mileage out of choices that inform your audience about your:

- Gender.
- Sexual orientation.
- Age.
- Familial relationship.
- Location.
- Time.
- Events (past and future).
- Profession.
- Condition (drunk, stoned, injured, ill, mentally impaired).

Let's look at another performance. Jodie Foster won the Academy Award for Best Leading Actress for her 1988 role in *The Accused.* In this film, she plays a rape victim. She's a working class woman, a waitress, who before the first scene even takes place has been gang raped in a bar on a pool table by two men while a group of other men cheered her attackers on. In the first scene she runs out of the bar barefoot and screaming with torn clothing and scraggly hair. Next we see her in the hospital. When she speaks, it is with a husky voice. (A choice that has to do with the screaming? With the bruises on her neck indicating she was choked during the attack?) She has a blank expression on her face. (A choice demonstrating shock?) Those choices reveal her condition.

There is a clear class distinction between her character and the character of the deputy district attorney assigned to her case (played by Kelly McGillis). This distinction is evidenced by their clothing (jeans and a sweatshirt vs. a business suit) and speech patterns (regional lower-class accent vs. neutral middle-class accent). Foster's state of mind is revealed also by behavioral cues. For instance, when the DA is driving her home, her eyebrows are raised in the middle like a lost little kid. This makes her come across as forlorn and confused. It helps us to view her as uneducated, naïve, and defenseless.

At home in the trailer park, in a scene alone, Foster is seated on her bed. She holds herself in a ball with her arms wrapped around her knees, hugging them towards her chest. Her behavioral choice is to rock herself as if she's rocking a baby to soothe it. Those choices show us her mental and emotional condition (wounded, vulnerable), and also something about her character's lifestyle (isolated, self-supporting).

Scene by scene in a film like this, the character develops. As an actor, you would map out this journey for yourself, and then make choices for where you are on the trajectory mentally, physically, and emotionally. But in a given scene, as in a single scene from an audition, you only need to represent where you are in that specific moment.

Playing Your Obstacles

Physical conditions, such as being drunk, crying, and having an asthma attack, are obstacles that you have to adjust for behaviorally. To play drunk, you could imagine that everyone around you is very hard of hearing, and then let this affect your actions. Wheezing might be like drowning. If you lacked oxygen what would that be like for you? Let your character's condition serve as an obstacle to accomplishing your objectives.

To play blindness, try letting your eyes slip out of focus, and overcompensate for your lack of vision by concentrating intently on every sound you hear. Watch Al Pacino's Academy Award-winning performance in *Scent of a Woman* (1992) and observe how he portrays his character's physical condition as a blind man.

Russell Crowe's portrayal of scientist John Nash in the 2001 film *A Beautiful Mind* (scripted by Akiva Goldsman) earned him an Oscar nomination. With scenes spanning the years between 1947, when Nash entered graduate school, and 1994, when he won the Nobel Prize, Crowe had to track elements of Nash's physical condition, modifying and magnifying them according to his mental and emotional state, as well as his age. Nash is portrayed as a genius lacking social skills and suffering from paranoid-schizophrenic delusions. Until the midpoint of the movie, the audience doesn't suspect that the people with whom Nash is interacting are figments of his imagination. We see them as he does. After the veil of his delusions is lifted, from then on we are actively looking for Nash's moments of sanity and insanity. Crowe has several scenes interacting with phantoms, where no one else is present in the shot. This work is very specific.

Crowe's physical adjustments include ways of moving that showed him advancing from youth to middle age to old age; vacillating between sanity and mental illness; and also representing introversion and flashes of genius. When he's speaking with most people, he hesitates to look them in the eye, often only shooting darting, sideways glances at them. He keeps his fingers curled inwards, like he doesn't want to touch anything, and often keeps his hands in his pockets. He often holds a briefcase in front of him, as if to protect himself from a frontal assault, or like a child clutching a teddy bear. When he's describing scientific insights and thought processes, he put his hand to his forehead and points outward from there in abrupt gestures while saying his lines, as if literally pushing thoughts outward from his brain.

When Nash is in the throes of his delusions, Crowe has uncombed hair and wears untidy and mismatched clothing. He hunches over. When his mind is clear, his hair is neatly combed and his clothes fit well. In these scenes, his ties are correctly tied, rather than missing or misaligned. His posture is upright. Crowe found an unusual gait for Nash where he takes small, jerking steps. In the scenes from his youth, this seems naïve and childish. As the character ages, this manner of walking becomes more pronounced, and looks both like an infirmity and like he lacks conscious connection to his body.

There are also scenes in the film where Nash is heavily medicated and it's scripted that he is unable to think with the clarity necessary to "do his work." Crowe shows his emotional state of depression and hopelessness through a lack of movement. There's one scene where Nash is holding his infant son, who is fussing, as if the boy is a sack of potatoes—meaning, with no responsiveness, like Nash has become frozen in place.

Conditions that represent obstacles for your character can be conditions of mind, heart, or body. In each scene, you must know where your character is in the trajectory of his or her experience, so you can purposefully track the physical adjustments. In shooting a film, plotting this out ahead of time is essential, because film scenes are generally shot out of order. For an audition, you take the given circumstances in the script and choose the specific adjustments that show you understand important dimensions of the character, and what you would likely do with those adjustments were you cast in the part.

 Tip for Playing Evil

If your character is supposed to be evil, play the body language of *delicious*. Watch Christoph Waltz's Academy Award-winning performance as the Nazi colonel Hans Landa in *Inglourious Basterds* (2009) to see how gleefully, how *deliciously*, he plays the role of the film's arch villain.

Contrast his way of doing that role with Glenn Close's as Cruella De Vil in *101 Dalmatians* (1996), a very mean performance that, in my opinion, was not much fun to watch, though she received an Oscar nomination for it nonetheless. Anger and meanness are less captivating than evil that includes a degree of narcissistic self-satisfaction. The physical adjustment of evil actions can be like the physicality of indulgence in food.

Muscle Memory

Memory is stored in the physical body. When motions and gestures are repeated, a memory is created inside the muscles for the task so that it can be repeated automatically with little or no conscious effort. This is obviously true for such activities as riding a bike or playing the piano, but it is also true for the way people walk and sit and eat. Did you ever see the Charlie Chaplin movie *Modern Times?* Set in a factory, there's a hysterical scene in which Chaplin steps away from an assembly line where he's been turning bolts with a wrench for hours. His right arm keeps bolt-turning in the air spontaneously like he's got a twitch. It's muscle memory taken to an absurdly extreme degree.

The interesting thing about muscle memory is that if you change your physicality or repeat certain gestures to match the body language of a particular character, you begin to experience how that physicality makes you feel and think. When images come to the surface of your mind through the influence of certain physical behavior, that's where you can find those terrific As Ifs like, "I'm a dog with fleas." Scratch yourself and see what it evokes in you if you combine the gesture and the mental image of the dog.

How would you behave if you'd been shot in the leg? Unless this happened to you, you can only compare that condition to other experiences your body has actually lived through and remembers. (This might come up in the script for an action movie or a cop show.) *Humanizing* works in the rehearsal process for conditions as well as it does in rehearsing clichés. Talk aloud to yourself. "Shit! That burns! It stings so bad!" As you speak aloud respond physically to what you're saying and see where it leads you. Do you grab your leg? Do you wince? Does your breathing change? Do you tense your jaw? Bite your lip? Lift your shoulders? You may find some usable body language for the scene you're preparing for your audition by playing around with conditions given in the script.

Highly emotional events, both positive and negative, and traumatic events tend to be more memorable than commonplace events. Affective memory, also known as *emotional memory,* is the technique of calling up past events from your life that are comparable to a character's and flooding your body with those emotions to evoke the body language. This is another way of bridging the life of the character to your own life. Always remember that the body language has to read on camera. Once you've found it in rehearsal, craft it specifically by making a choice. You can trust that your body will recall it. Do the behavior and the emotions will follow.

More than once I've advised a student who needed to cry on cue just to start doing the physical behavior of crying and let the reality kick in. This really works: The behavior reads as truthful. If you don't believe me, go and look at footage from the murder trial of Marlon Brando's son. When Brando testified on behalf of his son, at one point Brando turned away from the judge and behaved as if he was crying, but I think you can see it was a put-on. From the judge's perspective, however, it looked real, and he believed it. You can do the same thing with laughter. Start laughing, incorporating all the accompanying behavior, and the emotional reality of laughing will be generated by your body's muscle memory.

Social dictates must be expressed in body language; otherwise no one can read them. The physicality of a Victorian lady in society was a highly elaborate code that both women and men understood. Years ago, on the back of a postcard I received from the Oberon Theatre Ensemble advertising a production of *Lady Windermere's Fan* by Oscar Wilde, was a list of Victorian hand fan gestures and their meaning. It was so fascinating that I saved it for over a decade. There were gestures involving closed fans, open fans, speed of fanning, right hand, left hand, and more. You can find lengthy, detailed lists like this online by searching the phrase "Hand fan language." Just to give you a taste of how specific and complex this female body language could be:

- Resting the fan on the right cheek meant, "Yes."
- Resting the fan on the left cheek meant, "No."
- Pressing a half-opened fan to the lips meant, "You may kiss me."
- Touching the tip of the fan with a finger meant, "I'd like to speak with you."
- Drawing the fan across the eyes meant, "I'm sorry."

Watch Gillian Anderson's performance in *The House of Mirth*, directed by Terence Davies from a script by Terence Davies, which was adapted from the famous novel *The House of Mirth* by Edith Wharton. A story about social manners within the British upper class at the turn of the twentieth century, her character, Lily Bart, is disgraced because she is unmarried and foolishly does not protect her good name. You can see how restricted Lily's choices are as a woman without means of her own participating in high society of this period. She makes mistake after mistake and ultimately comes to a tragic end. Anderson embodies the social dictates of the period very specifically.

Military personnel also use hand gestures as a silent code when they're on a mission and don't want to be discovered. Japanese businesspeople have special ways of bowing and exchanging business cards when being introduced to people of different stature. Many groups use encoded body language to communicate. Though at some point people may be directly taught the codes, the stylized behavior becomes so engrained in them from living in the social groups where they live that it becomes automatic. If you're going to use it, practice it so that it becomes stored in your muscle memory.

You Are in Charge of Your Instrument

You are an independent producer. You possess an instrument, like a flute or a guitar, which is a composite of your body and voice. And you take this instrument wherever you go and produce events that feature it. You act. So though you are not the producer of the project you're trying out for, you are the producer of every audition you perform.

As the owner of the acting instrument, it is your responsibility to properly maintain your voice and your body. You can do this by staying healthy, flexible, and fit. An actor who has laryngitis can't perform. An actor who is out of shape doesn't have stamina. The skin of an actor who wakes up every morning with a hangover usually looks like crap.

It is also your responsibility to practice using your body and voice so that you know what they're capable of doing. In other words, commit to studying and mastering your craft, and work to understand and expand your dimensions as a human being. It's wise to rehearse in advance for the kinds of parts you can imagine being cast in. There's an old adage that applies: Success is opportunity meeting preparedness. Be prepared.

Surely you can recall watching interviews with actors describing how they learned to ride a horse, drive a racecar, box in the ring, dance tango, play trumpet, or sing country music songs in order to meet the demands of roles they'd been cast in for various films. Training in specific skills, like martial arts, can make you a more appropriate choice for certain parts. Of course, in the audition room, those types of activities are rarely called upon. You're seated and they're interested in your ability to generate reality. However, if the role is an athlete and you've got a potbelly they won't be able to see you in the role.

The kind of research you could do for an audition has more to do with taking the clues from the script, understanding them, and determining how to embody them. If you know who you are in your natural state, you are on the road to knowing when to leave yourself alone and when to make a change. You may already be close to the character.

Take Wendie Malick as an example. She was one of my students years ago. She was always fun to work with, and enjoyed acting. She had started her career as a Wilhelmina model, and then got recognition playing the sinister, other-woman type because of her arched eyebrows, dark hair and eyes, deep voice, and statuesque appearance. She'd finished studying and was working, but was not yet a hot property back then. Comedic roles came after she discovered her fun side. Then casting directors discovered her quirkiness, too. In 1997, she got cast as a parody of herself in the role of Nina Van Horn, a dark-natured model, in the TV sit-com *Just Shoot Me!*, a role for which she won an Emmy. Since then she's been working non-stop in all different kinds of roles. At the present she's a big hit in *Hot in Cleveland.* In that show her character's name is Victoria Chase, a man-chaser. Talk about a perfect name for Sherlock Holmesing!

Johnny Depp is an example of someone who makes chameleon-like character adjustments. He's brilliant at tapping into his imagination. Just think of his role as Captain Jack Sparrow in the *Pirates of the Caribbean* franchise, where he's emulating Keith Richards . . . but on steroids. He started his career playing a pretty boy cop on the TV show *21 Jump Street.* Not a big stretch of the imagination. But that opened doors for him. After realizing his knack for making extreme adjustments, he then made it a kind of personal mission never to repeat his characterizations.

Watch Depp's physical and vocal adjustments in the 1997 film *Donnie Brasco* (scripted by Paul Attanasio), where he plays an undercover FBI agent who infiltrates the Mafia. As time goes by and Brasco immerses himself ever-more deeply in the crime family, his appearance and mannerisms evolve. He takes on the life of a "made man." Depp's work in this film is an example of how an actor must be super-specific in every scene.

Remember, a label is not a fence. It's a doorway. Use the labels for the types of characters you get a chance to audition for to open new worlds of possibility for you as an actor. When you meet someone with a Ph.D., or a chef, or a writer, for instance, get curious. Ask, "What can you teach me about that?" Set aside your preconceived opinions about people and open your mind. Be an observer. Watch what they do and how they do it, and listen to how they say what they say. Rifle through the filing cabinet of your imagination to find the physical and vocal truth of your character's unique humanity, as you interpret it. As long as the script supports your choices, they're okay.

Human behavior is idiosyncratic and frequently peculiar. Seven billion people are living on the planet and each of us behaves in certain ways for certain reasons; this puts a lot of potential physical and vocal adjustments on the "menu" for actors. Don't be afraid to be "strange," for, as has been said, the truth is often stranger than fiction. Try to catch yourself and the people around you doing things truthfully in an interesting way.

Notes

CHAPTER 13
ACTIONS

In order to perform an action truthfully—and therefore convincingly—an actor needs to find exactly the right action to suit that particular situation and that particular line."
—Marina Caldarone and Maggie Lloyd-Williams

Acting is *doing combined with emotion.* Human beings do what we do because of how we feel. That's why I've repeatedly recommended that you begin your crafting of a scene by determining the feeling you must generate to reveal the character's truth. That feeling should—and will—dictate your choice of action in every beat of the scene. Never forget, every single action must be demonstrated by physical behavior. It is not effective to name an action—even an intention inside a character—that cannot be seen by the camera.

Every action has an inherent point of view. An action is not something that's thought up or invented. It is determined by looking closely at the clues you found in the script pertaining to people, places, things, and events. Once you understand the truth of the moment from your character's P.O.V., you then select actions. At the end of the day, it doesn't matter what you *call* an action just as long as you *know* what it is.

There are a lot of actors who know how to act competently. The trouble is that there are not as many actors who know *what* to act. Choice of action does not come from what you say. Acting has little to do with talking. Stick with behavior. If an action cannot be shown, then it's not real to the viewer. Every action must be physically expressed.

You also need to trust that pursuing one action is enough. The road to hell is the idea "I've got to do more." One of the problems inherent to being an actor is that you have too much information—much more than you normally would about the people and events taking place in your real life. You have to stay rooted in the present reality of the scene. Do not aim to foreshadow knowledge that your character does not yet possess. That is the character's future, so it is unknown. Don't try to play the whole scene at once, or the whole film or TV episode; rather, figure out what action you are doing *right now.*

What Is a Beat?

For the purposes of the on-camera audition the definition of a *beat* is this: When you are doing one thing (an action) one way (an emotion) for one reason (an event) in order to get what you want (that which you want the reader to understand about you). This defines *how* you play a beat.

A beat covers the space of one thought and one action. Don't try to do two things on the same beat. Be simple. Trust your choices. Play your scene one beat at a time.

Also don't take on the burden of trying to make a lousy script good by complicating your actions. There are plenty of poor scripts out there. Just deal with the reality of the situation. If the script is rotten, aim for clarity rather than complexity. Act a cliché.

The duration of a beat may be short or long depending on the script. A beat is simply the length of time you pursue the same action in order to get what you want overall. In film and TV, scenes are one or two beats at most with rare exceptions. Beats generally change only because of something the object of your attention says or does, or because you discover new information from some other source.

Finding Your Actions

In looking for elements of behavior, for the actions to play, begin by asking, "What would this situation be like for me?" Break down your character's actions in the script. Human beings are always feeling something. This emotion is always the result of an event that either has occurred in the past or that we anticipate will occur in the future. The past could be just a minute ago. The future could be just a minute ahead. Because of this event causing us to feel a certain way, we do something in order to get what we want. Use the same action until you are forced to change it by what occurs in the script.

Your action is not merely to express the character's emotion. There are always reasons to be emotional. Know those reasons, and then use them to define your series of actions. Know your objective in the scene, which is only ever one thing. This is so even in scenes where there are several actions that move you toward your goal. The action always comes from the script, out of the relationship and what you want.

What are you doing (your action)? Example, "I'm putting my foot down." This action underlies everything you do and say until your character cannot pursue it any longer.

In acting, you work from the verb that best describes what you're doing in regards to the other person. Possible actions are verbs like:

- Tease
- Threaten
- Seduce
- Dismiss
- Admit
- Recall

An action can be a byproduct of a social dictate. Therefore, when you're doing character work, always remember that people are what they do. For instance, a magazine editor *corrects.* A judge, *judges.* A lawyer *negotiates, argues,* or *persuades.* Socially dictated actions will always fall into the range of possibilities for your character.

In *The Good Wife* (CBS), for instance, Juliana Margulies' attorney character often *waits,* whereas Chris Noth's politician character typically *seduces.* In *Dexter* (Showtime), Michael C. Hall's serial killer character *calculates, plots,* and *plans.* In *The Big C* (Showtime), Oliver Platt's estranged husband character *begs* and *appeases.* In *Breaking Bad* (AMC), Bryan Cranston's chemistry teacher-turned-methamphetamine dealer character *solves.* In *Damages* (FX/ Audience Network), Glenn Close's high-powered attorney character *congratulates* herself over her power.

The action verb becomes informative or entertaining through *how* you do it. There are a lot of different ways for your character to threaten or beg or admit. You can discover those particular ways during your crafting process by day-dreaming and humanizing.

To find your actions, don't worry so much about the actual lines. Just free associate and improvise around how your character is feeling and you'll naturally understand what the character is doing. This practice will connect you to the reality of the story. You can begin by taking the point of view of the title you've given to the scene.

Let's say the title of your scene was "Never Again." Your humanizing would sound like: "I am so pissed off at her. I cannot believe she said that to me. How dare she?! I am going *to teach her a lesson* when I see her. I am going *to tell her off* and, in no uncertain terms, I'm going *to set her straight* that she can *never again* speak to me that way." The reason your actions are "teach her a lesson," "tell her off," and "set her straight" is that you want her to understand that you are *not going to stand for this anymore.* Please notice that all of the chosen actions had to do with the reader and what you want her to understand.

For preparation right before an audition, you can humanize your dialogue in the same manner while you're in the waiting room—being particularly mindful to reiterate and reinforce the actions. Whenever you rehearse, it's a good practice to do things bigger than normal. This will help you to anchor your specific choices in your muscle memory.

Never pantomime an action. When a physical action that requires a prop, like lighting a cigarette, is described in the script, don't fake that action. Miming robs your actions of their truthfulness on camera. Instead stay focused on the reader, as that's the direction in which the camera is located, and do the action that moves your character toward the fulfillment of the question "What do I want this person to understand about me?"

When a script gives you an intricate activity to do while dialoguing, such as putting coins in a snack machine or mixing chemicals in a laboratory—something that in the actual filming would require your character's intent focus—it means that while you're doing this physical action you are supposed to throw away the dialogue, to just spit it out. In an audition room, it is, of course, not possible to do such an action, nonetheless you must say the lines in an offhand manner to show the producers that you understand what's happening at that moment in the script. Blow through it so you can get back to the next, more central emotional action that involves the reader.

The Crucial First Moment

You must be immersed in the reality of the scene when the scene starts. Auditions are frequently won or lost in the first moment. It's critical to craft this moment specifically. If you don't know the object of your behavior and what you want this person to understand about you, your boat is going to be dead in the water from the start. The first moment depends on the given circumstances. Those are non-negotiable.

Everything I train actors to do is to get you ready for the first moment: Sherlock Holmesing the text; clichés; expletives; personal reasons to feel as you do about people, places, things, and events in the script; physical and vocal adjustments; social dictates—these are all essential for taking off with a roaring start in the first moment. If you get that first moment down pat, then the rest of the scene is just making the beat changes where they're called for, and talking and listening to the reader.

When you go to your audition, talk to the producers like human beings. If a script says sit, sit. If it says stand, stand. If there is a chair in the audition room and the script says to first stand and then sit, ask if the camera will follow you on that particular line. This is information you need so that you will remain in focus as the camera follows you. Keep things simple so sitting down or standing up is part of the action you are playing. Actors must move for a reason. If you can avoid sitting down or standing up in the middle of your scene, it keeps things lean and simple.

For auditions, avoid entrances at all costs. An entrance is really an exit from someplace else. You can achieve the same vitality as if you had just walked even though you're already there. My proof of this is the fact that quadriplegics can act. Christopher Reeves acted very well in the 1998 remake of *Rear Window* after he'd had the horseback riding accident that paralyzed him.

In a film or television scene, an entrance is the way that your character comes from a place where something specific has happened to the only place that he or she could come to accomplish a specific goal. The scene takes place here because of what happened in the other place. An exit is exactly the opposite. Because of what has just happened in this place (the scene) your character is going to the only place he or she could go right then.

Watch Michael Douglas's performance in the 1994 thriller *Disclosure,* directed by Barry Levinson, to see how specific entrances and exits can be. Many times he walks in and out of his character's office. Each time he enters or exits, Douglas does it a little bit differently because of what has just happened.

Also watch Alan Rickman's entrances and exits in the 1995 film *Sense and Sensibility*, directed by Ang Lee. His character, Colonel Christopher Brandon, repeatedly comes to visit Marianne Dashwood (played by Kate Winslet), each time arriving and departing in a distinct way depending on what has just happened.

A Beat Alone

If the reader has the first line of dialogue, then you are having what I term a *"beat alone."* This becomes the first moment of your scene. On a beat alone, you have three choices of action, as follows.

- *Choice 1:* Praying. (Really pray)
- *Choice 2:* Figuring out. Figure out what kind of makeup you would put on the reader (work off of the person in front of you so that your action can be captured on camera) or add up the ages of the members of your family. Specificity reads in an actor's behavior and facial expressions
- *Choice 3:* Recalling. (Try to hear the sound of your door closing or the sound of your heart beating)

For the sake of clarity, do not try to combine these three choices. Pick one option off the menu of options and do it wholeheartedly. Do it for real.

Jack Nicholson was working on a close-up once for a beat alone and afterwards the director said, "Man, that shot was amazing! What were you doing?" Nicholson replied, "I was counting parking meters." Counting is a truthful action that the audience can see on screen, and will interpret in terms of your character's situation. Another thing you could do besides counting parking meters is to try to recall every telephone number you've had in your lifetime. People will watch what you do, so long as you do something real.

 ## Tip for How to Play a Memory

On camera, when the script calls for it, you can reveal that you're engaged in the act of remembering something by listening for a real sound. A way to practice this is by trying to hear the door of your apartment or your house closing—if you know how far away your apartment or house is from where you are seated. A long ago memory is a function of distance. Another option is to replay an actual memory of the sound of a screen door opening in the house where you lived as a child or of a squeaky bicycle wheel you once rode. The farther back in time the memory of a sound you use is, or the further the distance you are away from the sound you are trying to hear, the farther back in time the memory will appear to come from in your scene.

The camera does all of the work for you when you are having a real memory or listening for a real sound, even if it's not exactly parallel to the line of dialogue you're saying or hearing. An actor's job is to go from the general to the bspecific and from the complex to the simple. So reveal thinking and *be* thinking, and your audience will entirely believe in your reality.

A beat alone can be any scene where your character is alone. Watch George Clooney's riveting scene where he's seated alone in a taxicab at the end of *Michael Clayton* (2007). He actually seems to have several different alone beats. You can really see him thinking. It goes on for a couple of minutes, and it's never boring.

In an audition, you may ask the casting director or producer if it's okay to start with the first line of your own dialogue if you do not want to take a beat alone. That first line can serve as your beat alone, even though it's said out loud to someone else.

On companion DVD 2 to this book, you can watch actors demonstrate the three choices described above. Go to: TimPhillipsStudio.com/dvd.

If You Are Given an Adjustment

Let's say you do the scene once. Then the casting director turns to you and says, "Let's do it again, but this time do it with more menace *[or fill in the blank]*."

The best way to handle an adjustment, if you are given an adjustment of any kind, is simply to change your cliché, expletive, or action. For a stage audition, you would change your action. For film auditions it can be one of these three things. The verb is a choice, an interpretation. The director may have a different vision. He could be interested in how well you handle direction or what different emotional colors would look like coming from you. Or he might not know what he wants.

Keep the rest of the choices you crafted in place and make this one change and you will adjust easily.

The Decisive Last Moment

It's very important for you to do something specific at the end of the scene that demonstrates your character's point of view. Never let them see your energy fade out in an awkward moment where you shift to wondering if someone will say, "Cut." The Phillips' rule is to keep the life of your character going until the camera turns off.

In cases where the reader has the last line of scripted dialogue, you may choose to button up the scene by adlibbing one short line of dialogue. Clichés work well as buttons. If you got what you wanted make it a celebration. If you didn't, show how the character feels and thinks about it. Use the expletive for the reader. Use the title of scene. Just do something behaviorally so that the reader doesn't steal your focus at the end the scene.

Of course, you always want to be doing something for the benefit of the camera. But you also want to be genuinely absorbed in your interaction with the reader. That's why you must ultimately let go, trust that your choices are solid, and live the scene through from beginning to end, talking and listening as if it's the first time it has ever happened. How to talk and listen as an actor is the topic of our next chapter.

Notes

CHAPTER 14
TALKING AND LISTENING

❝ *Talk low, talk slow, and don't talk too much."*
—**John Wayne**

Talking and listening are the foundation of good acting. These elements are the "pinch" and the "ouch," a means by which actors can affect one another. How you say what you say, and how you hear what you hear, are your tools for creating shared reality, defining relationships, expressing feelings, and revealing knowledge. The conversation in a scene is a progression of moments that must be filled with life for the camera to capture. As an actor it is your job to provide the life underlying the lines—yours and the reader's.

Every fact you gleaned from Sherlock Holmesing a script and every tool of crafting you apply to a script that we have discussed thus far, from a scene title, a first moment cliché, expletives, and As Ifs, to a social dictate, physical adjustments, and actions, should be allowed to drop away the moment you are seated opposite the reader. If you have been thorough and specific, you can trust your body and mind to retain your crafting. Now, your purpose is to be human under these imaginary human circumstances. You are to experience the scene freshly, as if it is the first time you've ever said what you are saying and heard what you are hearing, and as if ignorant of what comes next. In the doing of the scene the text is of secondary importance to what is underneath it.

Emotion creates reality, and talking and listening reveal your emotions. If you have a feeling for something—a person, place, thing, or event—the camera picks it up. You do not have to indicate how you feel; don't aim to emote by furrowing your brow, moving your mouth, sighing, rolling your eyes, or putting a hand to your face. The "money" (aka the producers) won't be happy if you are indicating rather than listening and responding to the reader truthfully. The camera sees what actors know and feel, so being truthful is enough.

The Principia College Interview

In October 2007, Robert Duvall gave a one-hour talk to a group of acting students at Principia College, his alma mater. You can watch it on YouTube, as it was recorded. When asked about his process of acting, he said, "You can do all the intellectual concocting you want, but talking and listening is the beginning and end of acting…. These things can get emotional, or not emotional. You don't have to worry about it.

"You have to know your own temperament to be an actor," he elaborated. "To try to become somebody else, a character, is a trap. You *turn* yourself, as if you become a character, but it is still you operating. You only have one psyche, one imagination, one temperament, and that is what is *exploited*—in the good sense of the word. The idea of not knowing what is next is improvisation. With a script, you know what is next, but you try to go in not knowing what's next so that it is as if it's the first time you're doing it. You try to come in and delete the sense of relying on preconceptions. You stay in the moment. What's next? By improvising, you go in each time as if it's the first time you heard it. That's what the game is. It's a game. I talk, you listen. You talk, I listen."[1]

Later in the interview, Duvall explained, "You have to do research for whatever the part calls for, but when the time comes in a movie and they say, 'Action,' you have to throw away your preconceptions and all of a sudden go with the moment. See what they tell you and what you tell them…. If you are relaxed enough… if you are disciplined not to push, and stay in the moment, then you will be rewarded around the corner.

"Be open to what works, but go back to talking and listening, to the simplicity of that. It can get emotional without going for the emotion. Your imagination says, 'I think I can do something here.' But a line doesn't predetermine a way something should be said."[2]

Does this advice apply to an audition as much as to shooting a film? Sure it does. You have to honor the parameters within which you are performing, and yet you must also be open to your impulses and improvise truthfully. As Duvall says, "You need faith. Faith means believing in the situation."[3] Like a child, simply play. It's only make-believe.

Towards the end of the question-and-answer period of his talk, Duvall was asked about how he directs actors. He described feeling hesitant about giving notes when Miranda Richardson, an actress whose work he greatly admires, sought his direction on the set of *The Apostle*. He wrote, directed, and starred in that 1997 project. He told Richardson, "Nothing is precious. We don't have to get any place. We can go from zero and end at zero. Let the process take us to the result, rather than playing the result. Just start blank and end blank. If you don't put a burden on yourself, the scene will take its own way."[4] This approach exemplifies the underlying art of talking and listening.

Let's take a look at some other considerations in reading lines for an audition.

Working Off of the Reader

In Chapter 7, we explored the notion of a through-line. That's what you, as the character, want the other person (in an audition, the reader) to understand about you. It's the source of dramatic tension. Never forget that your reader is your reason for being in the scene, and you are going to create the magic circle of reality around one another.

When you are speaking your character's lines, you will know everything that you learned from Sherlock Holmesing the script about the words that you are saying. Through crafting around this knowledge, from personalizing this information in your imagination, you will have formed an experiential connection with your lines.

When you are listening, the same is true. Any time the actor opposite you is saying his or her lines, you will also have an experiential connection with those words—because you have Sherlock Holmesed them and then personalized them from the point of view of your character, ultimately bridging them with yourself.

Once you begin the scene, everything you do, you do to the object of your attention, for the object of your attention, or off of the object of your attention (the reader). You can trust that your crafting exists and will show up in your body because it is knowledge. Your mind/body does not know the difference between knowledge and memories you've imagined and direct knowledge. Both show up as real for the camera.

Over and over, I have advised my students to do less—just to talk and listen. You don't have to make an effort to hear the lines of the other actor. Just listen to them. Trust that your homework is there. If they don't believe me, I tell them to go get a camera and film themselves. See what they think of the results. You should do the same. Have friends over, and play around on camera and see what you can do in twenty-seven inches of space.

Acting on camera is like being a sniper on a mission. A sniper would never take his eyes off of his target; nor should you. Never look away from the reader (the object of your attention/object of your behavior) unless you are looking to a specific person, place, or object off-screen; or you are looking away—briefly and specifically—to reflect on a thought, engage in a memory of a historical event, or pray to God.

The Exceptions to the Never-Look-Away Rule: Memory, Mulling, and Prayer

Recalling a memory is an action that can be focused upon an object, or occur through a sideways glance. As we discussed in Chapter 7, time is an illusion of distance and looks like listening; see the tip on page 205.

We know from brain research that people's eyes move differently when they are remembering versus inventing an answer to a question. Have you ever seen the TV show *Lie to Me?* The lead character is an expert in neuro-linguistic programming. Among other things, he knows how to read certain indicators on a person's face that show whether or not they're telling lies. The funny thing is that we all can tell when someone is lying. It's a kind of natural human ability we have. By remembering a real sound, you avoid the problem of looking like you are *inventing* a thought.

When you're mulling something over in a scene, really mull something over. When you're praying, really pray to God. Acting is living a real human life for the camera.

On companion DVD 2 to this book, you can watch actors demonstrate praying, figuring out, and recall Go to: TimPhillipsStudio.com/dvd.

Do Something Real for the Camera

It's not "cheating," if your crafting gets results when it's not based on deep emotional preparation. You can put some real life in your eyes simply by doing something real, like counting the fence posts behind the actor you are listening to. This can be very interesting to watch. When we were shooting a scene from *The Lightship,* a crew member (the "focus puller") sat underneath the camera. He had an unusually long, red painted fingernail. I worked off of the nail as my focal point during my close-ups with Klaus Maria Brandauer that day because we were in a tiny space and Klaus was around the corner.

During my close-ups, Klaus was always trying to steal my focus. He'd be eating an apple or looking around aimlessly, trying to shake my concentration—doing anything he could to upstage me. But I didn't blink. I did my work because I am a professional. Studying that fingernail gave my performance reality since I was really doing something.

In the 2009 film *Get Low,* Robert Duvall has a scene with Bill Murray where, at one moment, he emphatically says to him, "Listen to me!" I would bet you anything that this was Duvall himself speaking to Murray, whose attention may have been wandering. It worked for the scene, so it made it into the final cut. Murray plays a mortuary owner. Duvall is an old man with a story to tell who wants to host his own wake and attend it.

Don't get too busy in an audition. It is your close-up. Simply let the reader's words and behavior push you around. The amount of anger you feel is not relevant to your crafting or to your performance. If the word "amount" is in your vocabulary, then it means you are going to push for a result, such as "a lot" of anger or "a little" anger. Pushing is a wrong choice. Trust your homework. Let your body and voice reveal the truth of the moment as it unfolds through you under your imaginary circumstances.

In a film, stillness is the way to get more close-ups. The viewers' connection to the other character is through you, and vice versa. That's why we need to see the other character's moments reflected on your face. Whenever the other character has a line, you can get a close-up by really listening to it and letting it affect you from your character's point of view. It makes the other actor's work seem better, too, if it affects you, so it's worthwhile for both of you if you are a generous listener.

One time, Sanford Meisner was portraying a bank clerk in the background of a scene. He got so caught up in his activity that one producer asked, "What the hell are you doing back there?" Meisner answered, "I am trying to make the perfect number seven." Since he was doing something real, it showed up as a mesmerizing action.

Scenes with Multiple Characters

A female student of mine was called in to audition for *Men in Black III*. From her sides, she saw that there were three people in the scene with her: her and the three leading actors. She asked me: "Where does one put all of those people?" This is what I told her.

If your audition scene is with two or more other characters, choose to speak your lines to the one that has the most responses to your lines. Deal with all characters other than the main one as one single person. The producer/writer wrote the scene, and the people in the room at your audition know the script, so you don't need to supply any information to them about there being multiple people in the scene with you. After all, they're not conducting a test of your ability to pantomime.

The only exception I can think of to this rule is when that other character—the one you are not focusing upon—has an important line. Be sure not to miss the types of lines that make the scene dramatic. If such a line occurs, turn your attention momentarily to a very specific place just to the side of the reader to say your line. Never forget that your eyes need to be captured on camera and it will be aimed at you from behind the reader. Once you establish this other person's presence always keep it in the same place.

Be mindful that your character may have different relationships with different characters. Allow what you know about those relationships to color the lines.

If you look away from the person you're speaking with during a scene in a film, that's the moment when the editor will cut away from your face to another shot. Audition tape is a close-up and you won't end up on the cutting room floor. But in the future, once you are cast in a role, remember that you can protect your work by not looking away.

Capturing the Moment No Matter What

Lauren Tom is an Asian-American actress, perhaps best known for playing Lena St. Clair in *The Joy Luck Club* (1993), although she works constantly on stage and screen. Back in 1988, stage director JoAnne Akalaitis cast Lauren as a motel desk clerk in the play *American Notes* by Len Jenkin, a role for which she received an Obie Award. In one scene, an actor came in as a mysterious guest. This particular fellow had a history of playing dangerous, mean men. He portrayed them so realistically that during the rehearsal period, Lauren called me up in a panic. She said, "I have to laugh in this one place, but I am so frightened of him that I just can't do it, Tim. I think I might get fired!" Lauren is a petite woman and she really felt intimidated by this guy. But she is also a pro and so knew she had to get that moment right. She just wanted to find a truthful reason to do it.

I told her not to worry, that we'd find a way to make her laugh. And we did. "When you get to this one line," I said, "I want you to imagine two flies fucking on the tip of his nose—literally imagine it." When she heard the suggestion, she started laughing so hard that she felt she had to pee. I remember she jumped up on the couch holding her stomach.

When Lauren won the Obie for that role she thanked me in her acceptance speech—although she didn't mention the reason why. But it was because she found a way to work off of the actor that broke through fear and shyness with him, and ended her intimidation.

Years ago, I had a female student who did a scene in a play with another actress who was being terribly rude to her. My student was seated on a bench, knitting, toward the front of the stage, where she was supposedly watching her kid at the playground. While the other performer was speaking she kept running around behind my student, trying to make my student turn upstage. My student stole the scene from her by commenting non-verbally—while remaining in character—on the lines. On one comment I remember how she blew into her cheeks, and puffed them up, like she just couldn't believe what she was hearing and rolled her eyes. All the while she kept knitting and listening, and facing forward. The audience ate it up.

The addendum to this story is that the other actress, who really wanted the play to be all about her, got very pissed off at my student. But there was nothing she could do.

Think of the scene from *Being Julia* when an aging diva named Julia (played by Annette Bening) takes over the stage during a younger actress' big monologue. She runs around in a costume that makes her look like a fluttering butterfly, overacting. It is a funny scene because it proves Julia's talent and ability to please the audience. In reality, the truth is that no matter what you do, you really can't upstage a good actor.

Here's another funny example of why never to mess with a professional. An aging grand dame of the theatre was being purposefully upstaged by a young ingénue. Tiring of this behavior, the seasoned professional took her glass of water and pushed it right to the lip of the table where she was seated. For the rest of the scene, the audience was entirely riveted on that glass, not the ingénue! Was it or was it not going to fall off the edge?

If you're faced with a reader who is trying to sabotage you, pull back and act the thought, "I can't believe what an asshole you are." Let the other guy hang himself. Be like Lois Lane: a reporter who's cool, calm, and collected. You're seeing the facts.

Pace Is Very Important

The impulse to respond to another character actually occurs somewhere in the middle of that person's line. It therefore must be connected to a rhythm that exists within the other person's dialogue. During an audition if you are looking down at your script for clues as to where this moment is, it signals that you don't yet know where that impulse to respond comes from. In my opinion, it comes from personalizing the script. Do your best to locate these specific important beats when you're crafting at home.

Overlap of lines can happen. This does not mean you should make a point to step on the other person's lines. It just means that you follow your impulse to respond. "Polite acting" is when you wait for the other person to finish before you begin to reply. In reality, we overlap one another when we're talking because of this impulse that arises in the middle of listening. *But it only happens if you know what you're hearing.* You only feel that natural urge to respond when the lines mean something to you.

The actors on the TV show *Parenthood* understand how to overlap their lines well. In many scenes, they are preparing meals for a whole family while carrying on a multiple-person conversation. The activity is making a meal, so many lines are tossed out rapidly. The dialogue is scripted to purposefully overlap in a naturalistic way.

You want to move quickly on the lines for the television. If you don't hit the comment or the joke immediately, the producers think you don't "get" it. However, you also need to give yourself time to have the moment. Let the other person impact you.

Actors often work too fast. By going for the results they're missing the journey. They miss living through the moments in the life of the character. When I see someone struggling with pace, my recommendation is that they play sports. Basketball is a good sport for actors, as are martial arts, like tai chi. These things help actors to stay present in the moment and find flow. Taking improvisation classes is another option. Improvisation helps actors to listen and collaborate to build a scene. It keeps moments fresh.

Put a "Button" at the End of Your Scene

It is okay to put a sound or a word or phrase at the end of the scene to sum it up in an audition. For instance, "I'm listening," "Spill it," "All right…," "Okay," "Prove it," or "Go for it!" If you don't have the last line in your audition scene, add on to it. Don't be afraid to improvise another word or two. My student Bruce Nozick took to this technique like a duck to water, booking twenty jobs out of thirty auditions, which is an amazing track record. Now he always buttons up the scene unless he's given the last line.

My student Michael Adler also had success with a button. In coaching him for his audition for the pilot episode of Jim Belushi's TV show *The Defenders,* for a role as a forensic pathologist named Dr. Pitts, I asked him, "What would you say to Belushi's character at the end of the scene if you could? He came up with, "This is not over yet." When Michael went in for the audition, Belushi was there. He loved Michael's button so much that Michael even got a second episode out of the character.

The lesson we can draw from this is the value of putting a button on an audition scene that implies something about the future. More examples: "We'll see about that." "You haven't seen the last of me." "I can't wait until the next time." Those kinds of phrases are especially useful. Also remember that any button you use must be a cliché, a human universal, or it won't work in your favor.

Producers in the casting session like it better when you end in a solid way, rather than having your energy dribble off as you wait for them to stop rolling. That's why it is acceptable to do this. Of course, you can't just say anything. It needs to be true according to the reality for the character in the moment.

Notes

CHAPTER 15

GRABBING YOUR LINES AND OTHER FUNDAMENTALS

> ❝❝ *We humans have a unique capacity to change . . . . We have tremendous adaptability, and with it come choice, intent, and full awareness.*❞
> —**Joe Dispenza**

Film is a technical medium. As an actor, you need to respect the constraints imposed upon you by the camera, and also to understand how to use them to your advantage. In addition, you need to adapt your performance, which is really just a reading of a script, to the setting of the audition room. Already we've discussed some of these fundamentals; now I'm going to suggest ways to practice them both on your own and with support from friends. The idea is to master the skills that will serve you well in an on-camera audition, and get rid of any poor habits you may have that detract from the quality of your work.

Let's begin with a basic auditioning skill, useful for on-camera or stage readings.

Grabbing Your Lines

In an audition, it is preferable to work from your script. Memorization is unnecessary. Nobody at an audition—not the casting director, not the director, not the writer, not the producer—expects you to know your lines by heart, and you will do yourself a disservice if you attempt to do an off-book audition unless you are a *really good,* quick study. There are only a handful of actors who can pull this off.

The exception to this rule of thumb is when you are self-submitting an audition video. Then, because you had plenty of time to do repeated takes, they do expect you to work without a script in hand. It should look more like a polished performance.

Typically if you memorize in a less than perfect way, when the camera lens captures the life in your eyes, everyone sees you trying to remember your lines—or else they see there is nothing in your eyes because you are terrified of forgetting them. And just imagine what would happen if you did forget a line. Stumbling with the words would override the crafting you prepared. No, you need to have the script in hand so that you can remain relaxed and refer to it before you deliver each one of your lines.

Holding a script in hand also relaxes the casting team. If you don't hold the script, they're watching to see how well you memorized your lines, which makes them acutely aware if you mess up. Wouldn't you rather they looked at other elements of your performance?

That being said, talking and listening are critical, for reasons we explored in the last chapter; as is keeping your face up and toward the camera with your eyes focused on the reader. The camera will be positioned and aimed at you from somewhere directly behind the reader. Your eyes are portals through which the viewer gains entry to your inner life. A piece of paper never gave anyone a job. Jobs come by way of the camera lens. Looking down at your lap literally shuts the door on the folks with the project and the money.

Moving between reading and being captured on film is a kind of a dance. How do you do the dance successfully? Simple: You must train for it. If you deliberately practice the skill of grabbing lines from reading material, you'll get better and better at it. Your brain will grow a new neural network for you connecting your eyes and your mind. Soon you can go from picking up one word or one phrase or one sentence at a glance to picking up whole passages of text. You'll also have a much easier time relocating your place in the script when you aim your eyes back down to the page. Just by practicing this skill for a few minutes a day, your proficiency with it will increase.

Here's everything you need to know to practice and develop competence.

1. Select any reading material: a book, a newspaper, a magazine, a script.

2. Pick a spot on the wall across the room from you—a specific spot.

3. Holding your reading material around waist height (which is below the level at which the camera will frame you during an audition), look down at the page. Read the first line.

4. Look up at your spot on the wall and say the line.

5. Look back down at the page, find the exact place you left off, and then read the second line.

6. Look up at your spot on the wall and say the second line.

7. Continue: Keep alternating between the page and the spot.

If you forget any line halfway through, simply glance back down to the page and locate the words exactly where you left off. At first you may not retain entire sentences. That's all right. This is something you do in the privacy of your own space when no one else is around and there is no external pressure being brought to bear on you. Soon you'll be able to grab bigger chunks of your lines at one go.

On companion DVD 2 to this book, you can watch as this exercise is demonstrated. Go to: TimPhillipsStudio.com/dvd.

Set aside a few minutes each day to practice grabbing your lines and your ability will improve. You'll mark a noticeable improvement and feel more comfortable holding your script in your hands when you're at your next audition, I promise you.

Refer to the Recommended Resources section at the back of the book for the URLs of online sources of actual scripts and sides to use in your practice sessions.

Less Is More: Acting vs. Schmacting

Remember, the camera sees what you know. If you have crafted an opinion about a person, place, thing, or event in the script—meaning you've personalized it and know how your character feels about it—then there is no need to work to indicate what you are feeling. Pushing is too much. In Yiddish, there is a great word for being excessively sentimental: *schmaltz.* Indicating is schmaltzy. Schmaltz + Acting = Schmacting.

Trust the clarity of your crafting to read on camera; and otherwise be still. Not frozen, but relaxed and responsive—like the human being who is living in the midst of a specific set of circumstances as provided by the script. Less is more when you're on film.

Being Still

A student of mine came to my tune-up class with the scene from the 1994 film *The Shawshank Redemption,* written and directed by Frank Darabont, where Red (originally played by Morgan Freeman) appears at a parole hearing. He has an impassioned dialogue about not knowing the true meaning of rehabilitation and remorse, but feeling regret and wishing he could go back to speak to his younger self and ask him not to make certain choices he did. These words finally secure Red's release from prison after forty years.

From across the studio, it seemed as if my student was doing too little. On screen, however, every nuance of his thoughts was captured and his performance was compelling to watch. That kind of acting for a close-up in an audition could get any actor hired.

You do not want to waste energy on movement that does not serve the scene. While you want life to flow through you freely and transparently, it is important to find your stillness and do nothing unless you have a specific reason to do it. Be simple.

When James Cagney was asked about his "school of acting," he said, "Plant both feet firmly on the ground, look them in the eye, and tell them the truth." And that's what I want you to do: Plant yourself in your chair, look the object of your attention—the reader—in the eye, and tell the truth.

The camera in an audition is in a static position; it is not tracking you unless you have prearranged for it to do so with the camera operator, who might agree for you to stand or sit on a specific line. Once the focus is adjusted, do not expect it to be readjusted. With the high-definition cameras that are being used today, even leaning forward a few inches can put you out of focus in the frame. And rapid gestures come out blurry. An audition is a close-up, so be relatively still and stick to showing what you know in your eyes.

Think about the difference between a home movie and a film. The home movie is more chaotic, isn't it? Professional film and TV is not shot in a chaotic manner. Except perhaps for an independent filmmaker who loves the handheld camera and is eager to play with it, you will rarely encounter a moving frame in an audition setting.

Voice and Speech

It is important for you to study voice and speech. Although with a microphone to pick up sound you do not need to project your voice, you still want to have vocal dynamics. You don't want to sound flat and monotone (unless it is a character choice) or to stumble over your words. You need to be understood.

If you have any question about how to pronounce a word, go to an online dictionary and listen to the sound of it. Most have auditory tools programmed into them. Know the difference between vocabulary words like *regimen* (as in diet or fitness) and *regime* (as in government), and that *nuclear* is not said, "nuke-you-lar," but "nuke-lee-ar."

Some parts call for regional dialects or accents. On *The Wire,* for instance, many characters spoke with a local Baltimore dialect. On *CSI: NY,* many speak with a local New York dialect. The same might be true for a TV show set in Boston or Atlanta. But not every character does. Expect the need for a special accent to be indicated in the character breakdown if it is a factor the producers are looking for specifically. If you often get called for specific ethnic character types, it's a good idea to work on these accents until you master them, so you'll have them in your "back pocket" ready to pull out.

Work on Your Chops

Even when you don't have an audition lined up or you don't yet have an agent, keep working on your craft every day. Take a yoga class, run some vocal exercises, watch a film by a director you admire, and read scripts. Most importantly, practice on camera.

Get yourself a Flip Camera or any other kind of inexpensive digital camera, and set it up on a tripod in your living room. Invite some friends over and take turns reading scenes with each other as if you were auditioning. Then watch the playback and make notes about what you need to work on to improve. Awareness is the best teaching tool. So be sure to make on-camera practice sessions a regular part of developing your craft.

Development as an actor takes time. There comes a day when the voice is dynamic, the body is dynamic, and a relaxed, grounded human being is captured on camera, living through moments from inside the reality. As long as you are still shifting outside of yourself in the midst of an audition to watch and judge and control your performances, this does not happen. Acting is so simple that most ordinary people find it challenging to be relaxed on camera. That's because you have to care about what you're doing and bring energy—vitality—to it, and yet not care. You have to be willing to be seen and heard, and to play unashamedly in your world of make-believe. You have to know the moments and then let go. It's like jumping out of an airplane. Once you jump, you should enjoy the flight because you can't go back—un-jump—you simply have to live it through.

The middle of the audition is not the place to second-guess your choices. If you have made strong, clear choices, acting will feel liberating and fun.

Rid Yourself of Bad Habits, Defensive Ticks, and Awkward Mannerisms

When we're nervous we all have little mannerisms that we use to fight against and dispel our uncomfortable feelings. These are things like jiggling a knee, fidgeting, blinking, looking away, or biting a lip. All of these mannerisms can destroy an otherwise good audition if they are allowed to persist.

In an audition, the frame of the camera is ribcage up, which is known in the trade as a 2-T (two-tit) shot. Actors do many things that do not translate well on screen in a 2-T close-up. Notice and then rid yourself of these bad habits, which include:

Too much hand action. Remember, it's what you know, and not how well you gesture, that matters. If you're waving your script or your hands around, this is going to detract from your scene work and draw focus away from your eyes.

Blinking. On screen, blinking translates to mean, "I don't know what I am seeing, hearing, or thinking." I am a big fan of the reality show *The First 48* (A&E). From that program I've learned that when suspects blink, the cops know that they are lying. So, unless there is a legitimate reason for your character to blink, such as telling a lie, avoid this behavioral tick.

Large-featured people, especially those with heavy eyelids, must be especially careful not to blink. The eyelids can look huge in a close-up shot.

For a model of how not to blink, watch Glenn Close act in *Damages.* She is living proof that you can train yourself not to blink for five minutes. If you have dry eyes, get eye drops. Just be sure the drops don't contain preservatives, because those can tinge the whites of your eyes red. Use enough to keep your eyeballs lubricated while you work.

Furrowing the brow. Scowling or holding tension in your forehead because you're "thinking hard" reads as over-the-top acting. It's too angry seeming. Keep your face relaxed and avoid any kind of pushing to indicate your emotions.

Popping the eyebrows. Some actors' eyebrows are constantly jumping around. Let your thoughts and emotions read through your eyes, not your eyebrows. If you have heavy eyebrows these movements can seem monstrously large in a close-up.

Looking away from the reader. Since the only reason to do the scene is for what you want this person to understand about you, you must never look away except to grab a line from the script. The only exception to this rule is to look away momentarily to a specific person or object. Review allowable exceptions in Chapter 14, "Talking and Listening."

If you do choose to look up or away on a line, be specific about where you look.

When you seat yourself, look up towards the reader. Cheat your body outwards a little bit so that the lens of the camera can catch your image better. In Michael Caine's book and video of the same name, *Acting in Film,* he explains how to do this well (see Recommended Resources).

Tipping your head forward or tilting it to one side. Until you see yourself on camera, you may not realize that you habitually tip your head forward or to one side when you are listening. In a close-up, it looks odd. This is not how normal people behave. And if you have heavy eyebrows or wear bangs you need to be extra careful about your head position, as you need to ensure you have light on your eyes so the producers can see what you know. Eyebrows and bangs can cast shadows.

 Tip for Correcting Posture

Yoga teachers always talk about imagining a string coming up out of the top of your head to hold your posture straight and elevate your spine. You can use the same visualization to practice no head tipping.

Squinting. Asian actors and those with narrow eyes must be careful to keep their eyes wide open during an audition. Work to reduce tension in your eye area so that when you get emotional your eyes remain visible. Squinting can be a form of indicating.

Biting the lips/frowning. Lip biting is another nervous gesture. The rule is: No face acting! Keep a relaxed face unless there is a character-appropriate reason to mug, such as Julia Louis Dreyfus's character does in *The New Adventures of Old Christine.* Making faces is a defining character trait and Dreyfus knows how to work successfully at this extreme.

 ## Tip to Overcome "Face Acting"

This is for actors who move their mouths and eyebrows too much. Scotch tape your eyebrows or around your mouth. Then, practice your lines. You'll soon feel when they are still. This is the cure for frowning and licking your lips excessively.

Licking the lips. If you feel nervous while auditioning, your mouth may get dry. Even so, licking your lips is something to avoid in a close-up. Apply lip balm and have a sip of water before you begin your audition if you believe dry mouth is a real problem for you.

Touching your face or hair. You don't want to have to keep reaching up and moving your hair out of your eyes. Leave it alone. Otherwise the scene becomes about that. Putting a hand on your face or over your mouth is a poor choice, as it only serves to hide your emotions from the camera.

As a general note on appearance, it also wouldn't hurt for you to fix the condition of your teeth if they're in bad shape and to wear contact lenses for on-camera auditions. In a close-up, your mouth and eyes are in the spotlight, so to speak.

On the Subject of Props

The only prop that is appropriate for an audition is a cell phone, and only if it is called for in the script. A phone should never be used arbitrarily. And if you use a phone, keep aiming your face towards the camera so that your eyes can be seen.

I remember hearing about one guy who brought a gun to an audition. Big mistake! His reader that day had a job as a bouncer at one of the nightclubs downtown, so he instinctively took the gun off the actor when he saw the guy reach for it. He laid the actor flat out on the floor. Frankly, the actor was lucky he didn't get his arm broken by this security professional. The reader apologized afterwards for knocking him down, but it was really the actor's own fault for pulling out a dangerous-looking prop.

It is unnecessary to use props or to pantomime using props for the casting personnel. They are an educated audience and know exactly what the script says happens. And they are much more concerned with seeing how you hit the moments the writer gave you.

Never Apologize in an Audition

In general, if you blow a line, just keep going. Repeat the line you fluffed as your starting place. The only exception is if you are right at the beginning of the scene. Then you can ask for permission to start over rather than keep going. Just stop right away and say, "Excuse me, I need to start over."

An audition it is like a piece of music. If you don't hit the first eight bars, it is very difficult to finish the rest of the song. In the musical world, they wouldn't let you go on. In the world of auditioning for film and television, they allow you to continue. And you may be able to pull it out. Unfortunately, it is just as likely to throw you off course.

My student James DuMont has stopped a couple of times in auditions; and a few other times he wished he had stopped when he kept going despite having made a mistake. He says, "On occasion, I have regretted that I didn't stop. I know better than this. If you don't have that first moment clear, then you need to stop. Really, you win or lose an audition in the first ten to twelve seconds. So the first moment has got to be there. It's like telling a joke wrong. If you don't get the set up right, the punch line doesn't matter."

There's a caveat to this advice on starting over. Presumably you stopped because you didn't hit your first moment the way you planned it or you mangled the line. If you start over, you had best ensure that you do hit the first moment and lines well the second time. Nothing is worse than starting over and then doing exactly as you did before.

 Notes

EPILOGUE
NOW, GO DO YOUR WORK

> " *I've missed more than 9,000 shots in my career. I've lost almost 300 games. Twenty-six times, I've been trusted to take the game winning shot and missed. I've failed over and over and over again in my life. And that is why I succeed.* "
> —**Michael Jordan**

Paul Michael, founder of The Network in New York City, says that the top complaint he hears from the entertainment industry professionals who come through his studio is that as many as 90 percent of actors give poor auditions. Even if they're doing *something,* those who haven't been coached or taught to rehearse are usually doing the *wrong thing.* Choices are either nonexistent or inappropriate, or actors don't follow through on their choices to a sufficient degree.

Frankly, you can use the statistics to your own advantage. For if you make clear choices about how to do a role that bring a scene to life in your audition, you'll stand out as one of the elite 10 percent of actors who know how to deliver high-caliber work. Once you make a good impression, casting directors will put your name in their files as an actor that should be seen. You'll get called to audition more than before, further improving your odds of being cast.

Imagine being a producer auditioning fifty people. From the producer's point of view that is a terrible day of watching bad acting, if you see only one or two good scenes. Actors in the 10 percent elite will probably get something down the road from having done a good audition.

If you follow the advice I've given you in this book, you may soon find yourself seated in waiting rooms on a regular basis with actors with better credentials than yours, even "name" actors. That's what you want! It means you're doing something right. Whenever those seemingly impossible opportunities come up, focus on your Sherlock Holmesing, on your crafting, and on doing the best performance you can do. Do your best with each and every audition. Persistence pays dividends. Audition for your career, not for individual jobs.

If you find yourself negatively comparing your appearance against other people's—thinking "I have to be skinny" or "I wish I had more hair" —turn on your television and write down the names of all the actors you see in the programs you watch that look like you. Notice how many are skinny and how many are regular-sized people. Notice how many men have full heads of hair and how many have shaved heads or balding heads. You'll be amazed at how many *"yous"* you can find working in film and television. Someone is getting those parts—why not you?

In Los Angeles, one of my students decided she would make a point of meeting every casting director five times before she got started. She went to "Meet the Casting Director" type events every single week for at least a year, while continuing to study and practice her craft. When she started auditioning with an equal measure of commitment, the casting directors already knew her. She books work regularly and has a viable career now playing roles on TV and in films.

Anger, frustration, and jealousy are emotions you need to monitor in yourself. Back in the day, when I was still acting, I was brought in by a casting director to audition for the part of Sam Malone in the show *Cheers*. This was the part Ted Danson got. We had the same acting teacher, Ted and I. But I wasn't surprised or angry that he got the part instead of me, because you see, Ted was the "Aramis man." He was appearing in a lot of commercials right then and his face was plastered on billboards around Hollywood Boulevard. From modeling a men's fragrance, he was getting free publicity that had impressed the casting director. He was also right for the role.

Drop any anger you feel toward other actors and casting directors. It doesn't serve you.

Of course it stings when an actor who is obviously not as good as you gets cast instead of you. Just know that it's probably because the actor is friends with the director or sleeping with someone important to the success of the production. Another thing that might lower your anger level is checking out the person who won the audition, and what they've previously worked on. You may discover that they often come in a package with a writer or director. The same director, producer, and writer often work on every production together. They're a team.

The point is, don't give away your power during casting. Actors feel they have no control. I hear the same complaints today that I heard thirty years ago. You can complain and whine about the unfairness of the world, or you can win the battle with yourself. Your goal should be to walk out of every audition and say, "I did a damn fine job today. I did what I wanted to do." That's the reward you have control over. If getting the job is your main goal, then you may get upset.

You'll meet power hungry idiots, dolts, and so on. Maintain a healthy disdain for those types seated on the other side of the table at an audition. You are putting your artistry in their hands.

I believe every actor should do at least one play a year. Get your friends together, pour the coffee, and go to work as an actor in the theatre so you won't lose your soul to television. Also practice the techniques I've explained in this book until you can do them fast. And if you need more experience on screen, go do some films for graduate students enrolled in film schools. Those films have the same problems for an actor to solve as other films. Stretch yourself.

Casting directors and producers are praying more than you that your audition will go well. If you can, let them know to sit back, relax, and trust you, as you are there to solve their problem not to create new ones. Calm them down. Do your four pages and then go home. Check your ego and attitude at the door. When you are finished, grab your stuff and leave the room. Do not look for feedback. If you look at them they feel as if you are asking them a question. They feel obligated to comment. Unless they ask you to stay, do not stop to chat. Thank them and leave.

Be very careful about asking questions. I remember auditioning an actress once who was "right" for a part in a play I was directing. She asked me several questions that were answered on the very first page of the audition sides. Either she had read the answers and could not retain the information or she was trying to impress me with her inquisitiveness. Either way, she stood right against my table and asked, so I cast someone else. Stand back, and also do your reading and preparation. See if you can answer the questions for yourself before you arrive at the audition.

Fit the size of the room. If your scene is a high-intensity scene and the day is nearing its end, understand that the producers have been listening to heightened emotions all day long and may be feeling a bit beaten up. Modulate your tones. Do not abandon the intensity of your scene, but understand that it is the truth that matters. Yelling late in the day may be painful to hear.

Look at who was cast in the parts you did not get, then you'll begin to understand the reasons why a certain choice was made. Robert Redford knew that he was wrong for *The Graduate.* He reportedly said, "Do I look like a guy who couldn't get a date?"

Every day do three to five things for your career. Go to the gym, watch a good film, read a good book, look at a painting in a museum, and daydream. Daydream a lot. During pilot season actors with representation must be capable of doing many auditions in a day. You have to be able to work quickly by then, so you should practice your audition skills intently from June through December. Then your skills will be primed for pilot season, which runs from January through May. When things slow down for you, work like the dickens because you won't have time to work on your craft when you're busy.

My classes are always full during pilot season. And I always tell my students, "You should be studying when it's *not* pilot season!" Practicing your craft only in peak audition peri-ods is like being an athlete who only wants to play and doesn't want to train. Never skip a day. It wouldn't occur to dancers not to be in a dance class. I don't get this wait till the last min-ute attitude. Why not get really good at what you do mostly, which is audition? Why not get good at *that?*

If you've come this far, then you have already seen the light. I encourage you to keep studying, practicing, and mas-tering your craft so that you can blow away the competition.

Let me give you another sports analogy to inspire you to create rituals around your work. This is an anecdote about a golfer named Louis Oosthuizen, who won the Scotland Open at St. Andrews by seven strokes in 2010. That's a lot. Oosthuizen wasn't expected to win. He was good at the game, ranked fifty-fourth in the world. But there were many higher ranked golfers than him entered in the tournament. He shot a 65 on the first day, placing him in second place. On the second day, he took the lead with 67 shots, and never relinquished it. By the third day he was four shots ahead. Ultimately his final score was the second lowest in St. Andrews' history.

Each time Oosthuizen took a shot, he did exactly the same thing. Like a ritual. He stood, he put the ball on the terrace, he held his club out in front of him, and he looked at the hole. Then he took his shot. He never varied this behavior. It turns out he'd consulted a sports psychologist prior to the tournament on how to improve his concentration. He put a red spot on his glove that he used to initiate the pre-shot routine that helped him remain totally relaxed and focused when he swung his club. The results were so incredible that his world rank rose to fifteenth.

Epilogue

Please embrace the Sherlock Holmesing and crafting methods I've given you in this book and use them in a ritual way to prepare for your auditions. Do your prep in however much time you are given, make clear, specific choices, humanize before you go in, and then let it fly.

Now, go do your work.

Notes

END NOTES

Introduction

1. Michael Chiklis, as spoken to James DuMont and reported to me.

2. Malcolm Gladwell. *The Tipping Point: How Little Things Can Make a Big Difference.* New York: Back Bay Books, 2000.

Chapter 1: What's the Project Called?

1. David Chen. "A Letter from David Mamet to the Writers of 'The Unit,'" Slashfilm.com (March 23, 2010).

2. Ibid.

3. Ibid.

Chapter 4: What Has Happened Already?

1. Source: TV.com. Under the "Show" menu, search for "CSI: NY" and then check the episode listing for Season 3, Episode 3.

2. Source: Wikipedia.com. Search "Carbon monoxide."

Chapter 6: Who Am I?

1. Robert Wisdom interviewed by Neal Conan, *Talk of the Nation,* National Public Radio, May 19, 2010. Source: NPR.org/templates/story/story.php?storyId= 126977949.

2. Source: Wikipedia.com. Search "Prison Break."

3. Source: Internet Movie Database. URL: IMDB.com/character/ch0027670/bio.

4. John Kubicek, "Exclusive Interview: 'Prison Break' Star Robert Wisdom" (September 24, 2007), BuddyTV.com.

5. Neal Conan, *Talk of the Nation,* National Public Radio.

6. Ibid.

Chapter 7: What Do I Want this Person to Understand about Me?

1. Amy Dunkleberger, "The Basics of Screenwriting: Screenplay Structure and Visual Storytelling," Session 3 in an American Film Institute Course on the Fathom Archive (Columbia University, 2002). URL: Fathom.com/course/21701762/session3.html.

Part Two Intro

1. From a private conversation with Robert Duvall.

2. Jerry Orbach, spoken to Jeff Fasano and reported to my writer Stephanie Gunning.

3. Source: QuoteLucy.com.

4. Jason Robards. I believe this quote comes from a *New York Times* article, following his appearance in 1986 as Hickey at The Brooklyn Academy of Music.

Chapter 14: Talking and Listening

1. Principia College Robert Duvall theatre talk (October 19, 2007). Video posted on YouTube. URL: YouTube.com/watch?v=3NQnjqMWGcs.

2. Ibid.

3. Ibid.

4. Ibid.

RECOMMENDED RESOURCES

Tim Phillips Studio
2124 S. Redondo Blvd.
Los Angeles, CA. 90016
(310) 772-8262
TimPhillipsStudio.com
Twitter: @TPhillipsStudio
Facebook: Tim Phillips Acting Studio

Selected Books

David Ball. *Backwards and Forwards: A Technical Manual for Reading Plays.* Carbondale, IL: Southern Illinois University Press, 1983.

John Basil with Stephanie Gunning. *Will Power: How to Act Shakespeare in 21 Days.* New York: Applause Books, 2006.

Michael Caine. *Acting in Film: An Actor's Take on Moviemaking.* New York: Applause, 1997.

Julia Cameron. *The Artist's Way: A Spiritual Path to Higher Creativity.* New York: Jeremy P. Tarcher/Putnam, 1992.

Harold Clurman. *The Fervent Years: The Story of the Group Theater and the Thirties.* New York: Harcourt, Brace, Jovanovich, 1975.

Harold Clurman. *On Directing.* New York: Fireside Books, 1997.

David Craig. *On Singing Onstage.* New York: Applause, 1990.

Malcolm Gladwell. *The Tipping Point: How Little Things Can Make a Big Difference.* Boston, MA: Little, Brown and Company, 2000.

Malcolm Gladwell. *Outliers: The Story of Success.* Boston, MA: Little, Brown and Company, 2008.

Malcolm Gladwell. *Blink: The Power of Thinking without Thinking.* Boston, MA: Little, Brown and Company, 2005.

Akiva Goldsman. *A Beautiful Mind: The Shooting Script.* New York: Newmarket Press, 2002.

Eva Le Gallienne. *The Mystic in the Theatre: Eleonora Duse.* New York: Farrar, Straus & Giroux, 1966.

Sidney Lumet. *Making Movies.* New York: Vintage, 1996.

Larry Moss. *The Intent to Live: Achieving Your True Potential as an Actor.* New York: Bantam Books, 2005.

Stephen Nachmanovitch. *Free Play: Improvisation in Life and Art.* New York: Jeremy P. Tarcher/Putnam, 1990.

Brian O'Neil. *Acting As a Business: Strategies for Success.* New York: Vintage, 2009.

Joseph Papp and Elizabeth Kirkland. *Shakespeare Alive!* New York: Bantam Books, 1988.

Sheri Sanders. *Rock the Audition: How to Prepare and Get Cast in Rock Musicals.* New York: Hal Leonard, 2011.

David Seidler. *The King's Speech: The Shooting Script.* New York: Newmarket Press, 2011.

Jill Bolte Taylor. *My Stroke of Insight: A Brain Scientist's Personal Journey.* New York: Viking, 2006.

Mark W. Travis. *Directing Feature Films: The Creative Collaboration Between Directors, Writers, and Actors.* Studio City, CA.: Michael Wiese Productions, 2004.

Selected Films and Television Shows

About Schmidt, directed by Alexander Payne. Script by Alexander Payne and Jim Taylor, adapted from a novel *About Schmidt* by Louis Begley. New Line, 2002.

The Accused, directed by Jonathan Kaplan. Script by Tom Topor. Paramount Pictures, 1988.

All My Sons, directed by Jack O'Brien. Script by Arthur Miller. Public Broadcasting System, 1987.

The Apostle, written and directed by Robert Duvall. October Films, 1997.

As Good as It Gets, directed by James L. Brooks. Script by Mark Andrus and James L. Brooks. Gracie Films, 1997.

A Beautiful Mind, directed by Ron Howard. Script by Akiva Goldsman, adapted from the biography of the same name by Sylvia Nasar. Universal Studios, 2001.

Catch Me If You Can, directed by Steven Spielberg. Script by Jeff Nathanson, adapted from a book by Frank Abagnale, Jr., and Stan Redding. DreamWorks, 2002.

Cold Mountain, written and directed by Anthony Minghella, adapted from a novel of the same by Charles Frazier. Miramax Films, 2003.

CSI: NY, "Love Run Cold." Script by Timothy J. Lea. CBS, 2006.

Disclosure, directed by Barry Levinson. Script by Paul Attanasio and Michael Crichton, adapted from the novel *Disclosure* by Michael Crichton. Warner Bros., 1994.

Do the Right Thing, written and directed by Spike Lee. 40 Acres and a Mule Filmworks, 1989.

Donnie Brasco, directed by Mike Newell. Mandalay Pictures, 1997. Script by Paul Attanasio, adapted from the novel *Donnie Brasco* by Joseph D. Pistone and Richard Woodley.

Falling in Love (1984), directed by Ulu Grosbard. Script by Michael Cristofer. Paramount Pictures, 1984.

A Few Good Men, directed by Rob Reiner. Script by Aaron Sorkin, adapted from his play by the same name. Columbia Pictures, 1992.

The Fighter, directed by David O. Russell. Script by Scott Silver, Paul Tamasy, and Eric Johnson. Paramount Pictures, 2010.

Fool for Love, directed by Robert Altman. Script by Sam Shepard. Cannon Group, 1985.

Get Low, directed by Aron Schneider. Script by Chris Provenzano and C. Gaby Mitchell. Sony Pictures Classics, 2009.

Good Morning, Vietnam, directed by Barry Levinson. Script by Mitch Markowitz. Touchstone Pictures, 1987.

Good Will Hunting, directed by Gus Van Sant. Script by Ben Affleck and Matt Damon. Miramax Films, 1997.

The Heiress, directed by William Wyler. Script by Augustus Goetz and Ruth Goetz, adapted from the novella

Washington Square by Henry James. Paramount Pictures, 1949.

The House of Mirth, directed by Terence Davies. Script by Terence Davies, adapted from the novel *The House of Mirth* by Edith Wharton. The Arts Council of England, 2000.

The Ice Storm, directed by Ang Lee. Script by James Schamus, adapted from the novel of the same name by Rick Moody. Fox Searchlight Pictures, 1997.

Inglourious Basterds, written and directed by Quentin Tarantino. The Weinstein Company/Universal Pictures, 2009.

The Insider, directed by Michael Mann. Script by Eric Roth and Michael Mann, adapted from an article "The Man Who Knew Too Much" by Marie Brenner. Touchstone Pictures, 1999.

Into the Wild, written and directed by Sean Penn, adapted from a novel of the same name by Jon Krakauer. Paramount Vantage, 2007.

Killer Joe, director William Friedkin. Script by Tracy Letts, adapted from his play of the same name. VVS Films, 2011.

The Lightship, directed by Jerzy Skolimowski. Script by William Mai, adapted from a novel of the same name by Siegfried Lenz. CBS Productions, 1985.

Michael Clayton, directed by Tony Gilroy. Castle Rock Entertainment, 2007. Script by Tony Gilroy.

Misery directed by Rob Reiner. Script by William Goldman, adapted from a novel by the same name by Stephen King. Columbia Pictures,1990

The Motorcycle Diaries (2004), a film from Argentina, scripted by Jose Rivera, adapted from both Ernesto "Che" Guevara's actual diaries and a book about his youth by Alberto Granado,

Please Give, written and directed by Nicole Holofcener. Sony Pictures Classics, 2010.

The Remains of the Day, directed by James Ivory. Columbia Pictures, 1993. Script by Ruth Prawer Jhabvala and Harold Pinter, adapted from a novel by Kazuo Ishiguro.

Saturday Night Fever, directed by John Badham. Script by Norman Wexler. Paramount Pictures, 1979.

Scent of a Woman, directed by Martin Brest. Script by Bo Goldman. Universal Studios,1992

Sense and Sensibility, directed by Ang Lee. Script by Emma Thompson, adapted from the novel *Sense and Sensibility* by Jane Austen. Columbia Pictures, 1995.

The Shawshank Redemption, written and directed by Frank Darabont. Adapted from the novella *Rita Hayworth and Shawshank Redemption* by Stephen King. Castle Rock Entertainment, 1994.

Sleepless in Seattle, directed by Nora Ephron. Script by Nora Ephron, David S. Ward, and Jeff Arch. TriStar Pictures, 1993.

Sophie's Choice, directed by Alan J. Pakula. Script by Alan J. Pakula, adapted from the novel *Sophie's Choice* by William Styron. ITC Entertainment, 1982.

The Trip to Bountiful, directed by Peter Masterson. Script by Horton Foote, adapted from his television play *A Trip to Bountiful.* Bountiful Film Partners, 1985.

United States of Tara, created by Diablo Cody and Steven Spielberg. Showtime, 2009–2011.

Venus, directed by Roger Michell. Script by Hanif Kureishi. FilmFour, 2006.

Online Practice Sides

ActorsPages.org/viewsides.php

Awesomefilm.com

Script-o-Rama.com

SimplyScripts.com

TwizTV.com

WhySanity.net

Additional Resources

Breakdown and self-submission service
ActorsAccess.com

Robert and Michelle Colt
ActingSuccessNow.com

Paul Michael's The Network
TheNetworkNYC.com

Shetler Studios and Theatres
ShetlerStudios.com

The Savvy Actor
TheSavvyActor.com

ACKNOWLEDGMENTS

All of the following people have brought me to the place in my teaching that I am, and were influential in the creation of this book. The absence of even one of these people would have made this book's existence impossible.

The first person I'd like to acknowledge is my grandfather, George Lozier, who demanded that I go to college. For always supporting my dreams, I'd also like to express my gratitude to my family: my mom, Maisie; my Dad, Ralph; and my sisters Betsy and Tammy.

My heartfelt thanks extend to:

Frank Galati, for dragging me on stage for the first time.

Carol Oditz, for seeing something in me that I did not see in myself.

Joanna Sexton, for seeing the actor in the bartender and demanding I go to class.

Sanford Meisner, for his invention of The Meisner Technique.

Robert Patterson, for putting The Meisner Technique into my bones.

Don Berger, for covering my bartending shifts so I could study.

Gale Youngs, for being a great acting partner and introducing me to Robert Duvall.

Robert Duvall, for treating me as a peer.

Gwen Cassel, for sharing in my dreams and supporting me in becoming a teacher.

Sir Arthur Conan Doyle, for creating the character of Sherlock Holmes.

Maggie Low, for being my teaching assistant and sitting behind me as my mind.

James Coyle, for endlessly transcribing recordings of my classes.

Jason Furlani, for giving me such wonderful plays to direct.

Emily Furlani, for designing my book cover.

Shaila Abdullah, for designing my book interior.

Larry Moss, for recognizing me in his book, *The Intent to Live,* and demanding that I come to Los Angeles.

Charlotta Nutley, for giving me two beautiful daughters and supporting my dreams.

My daughters Elssa and Sara, for giving me such joy in watching them play.

Polly Humphries, for helping the initial set up in Los Angeles.

Wayne Duvall, for letting me crash on his Los Angeles couch.

John Scott, for letting me crash on his Los Angeles couch.

James DuMont, for making my Los Angeles transformation a reality.

Rona Benson, for being my trusted Mac Genius.

Acknowledgments

Kat Jensen, for holding my hand when things got rough.

Robert and Michelle Colt, for opening my heart and mind to endless possibilities.

Sherri Snyder, for helping me compile lists of clichés for the book.

Ann Moller, for proofreading an early draft of the manuscript.

Allison King, for typing this.

Ron Shetler, for being a great new friend and allowing me to teach in his New York studios.

Paul Michael, another great new friend, for promoting me and allowing me to teach my New York intensives.

Richard Schiff, for being Richard Schiff.

My co-writer Stephanie Gunning, for seeing the book before I could.

Pablo Lewin, for his brilliant video work.

Last, but not least, I am grateful to the thousands of wonderful students I've taught over the years for teaching me.

ABOUT THE AUTHOR

Tim Phillips, founder of The Tim Phillips Studio, is an on-camera audition coach based in Los Angeles. A former actor and theatre director, in 1983 he established his studio in New York, where he taught principles of acting based upon The Meisner Technique. Since then, he has ignited the careers of Emmy Award-winner Richard Schiff, Emmy Award- and Golden Globe Award-nominee Wendie Malick, Nancy Travis, Roma Maffia, Robert Wisdom, and thousands of other actors. He has also coached Justin Timberlake, Molly Simms, Jayne Brook, Joanne Baron, Justin Chatwin, and Kate del Castillo. Tim has personally coached 35,000 auditions in the last twenty-five years. Over 70 percent of his students book roles from the audition scripts they bring into his class to prepare. Many of his current and former students have been casted as series regulars, recurring characters, and top-of-show guest stars on television and in feature films.

Tim's highly acclaimed Sherlock Holmesing the Text® method of script analysis is the foundation of his on-camera audition technique. In combination with his unique tools for crafting, his method is one of the most comprehensive and revolutionary approaches to auditioning ever made available to professional actors working in film and television. As a speaker, he regularly tours the country lecturing at colleges and universities.

For more information on Tim and his work visit: TimPhillipsStudio.com.

ABOUT THE WRITER

Stephanie Gunning is the co-writer or ghostwriter of over twenty-five books, including *Will Power, Rock the Audition, Audacious Creativity, You Are a Spirit, Total Renewal, Exploring Feng Shui, Easy Homeopathy, Whiff,* and *The Sedona Method.* As an editor and publishing consultant, her clients have included bestselling authors, like Gregg Braden and Hale Dwoskin, major publishing firms, top-caliber literary agencies, and innovative self-publishers.

Stephanie's career began at HarperCollins Publishers and Bantam Doubleday Dell. A freelance editor and writer since 1996, Stephanie, who holds a B.A. in English literature from Amherst College, now specializes in non-fiction books primarily in the areas of self-help, health, spirituality, and new thought. Books on acting are a subspecialty she particularly enjoys because for three years she was an actor. She is a member of SAG and AFTRA. At present she is at work on several writing projects on a variety of topics.

To write to Stephanie or to inquire about her writing services or speaking programs, please contact her through her website: StephanieGunning.com.

ALSO BY TIM PHILLIPS

Audio
Tim Phillips Studio Audition Technique (CD)

Video
*Tim Phillips' On-camera Audition Technique:
Sherlock Holmesing the Text® (DVD 1)*

*Tim Phillips' On-camera Audition Technique:
Crafting (DVD 2)*

Made in the USA
San Bernardino, CA
03 March 2019